NICK ARNOLD

illustrated by
TONY DE SAULLES

Scholastic Canada Ltd.
Toronto New York London Auckland Sydney
Mexico City New Delhi Hong Kong Buenos Aires

Scholastic Canada Ltd.
604 King Street West, Toronto, Ontario M5V 1E1, Canada

Scholastic Inc.
557 Broadway, New York, NY 10012, USA

Scholastic Australia Pty Limited
PO Box 579, Gosford, NSW 2250, Australia

Scholastic New Zealand Limited
Private Bag 94407, Botany, Manukau 2163, New Zealand

Scholastic Children's Books
Euston House, 24 Eversholt Street, London NW1 1DB, UK

Library and Archives Canada Cataloguing in Publication
Arnold, Nick
Fatal forces / Nick Arnold ; Tony De Saulles, illustrator.
(Horrible science)
ISBN 978-0-545-98535-2
1. Force and energy--Juvenile literature. I. De Saulles, Tony
II. Title. III. Series: Arnold, Nick . Horrible science.
QC73.4.A76 2009   j531'.11   C2009-901162-X

5 4 3 2 1   Printed in Canada   09 10 11 12 13

CONTENTS

Introduction   5

Nasty Newton   9

Forceful facts   26

Smashing speed   36

Gruesome gravity   52

Under pressure   69

Facts about friction   80

Stretching and straining   95

Getting in a spin   105

Bouncing back   123

Mighty machines   134

Build or bust   144

May the forces be with you   157

Fatal Forces quiz   161

Horrible index   171

Nick Arnold has been writing stories and books since he was a youngster, but never dreamt he'd find fame writing about Fatal Forces. His research involved falling off buildings, lying on a bed of nails and skiing uphill, and he enjoyed every minute of it.

When he's not delving into Horrible Science, he spends his spare time teaching adults in a college. His hobbies include eating pizza, riding his bike and thinking up corny jokes (though not all at the same time).

Tony De Saulles picked up his crayons when he was still in nappies and has been doodling ever since. He takes Horrible Science very seriously and even agreed to test what happens when your parachute doesn't open. Fortunately, his injuries weren't too serious.

When he's not out with his sketchpad, Tony likes to write poetry and play squash, though he hasn't written any poetry about squash yet.

INTRODUCTION

Science has one fatal flaw. It can be **seriously** boring. Ask a simple question and you're forced to listen to a really boring, complicated answer.

And some answers have masses of mysterious mathematics

And don't try arguing with a scientist either . . .

Or you'll get a forceful reply . . .

See what I mean? It's enough to make you die of boredom. Now that *would* be fatal.

* English translations:
1 Gravity is the force that pulls things down towards the Earth. The same force pulls a smaller object towards a much larger object.
2 The speed the ball falls depends on the strength of gravity. And this depends on the size of the Earth and your distance from the Earth's centre.
3 You're asking too many questions. I'll try blinding you with science.

So what are these laws? And what happens if you break them? Do you get expelled? Or perhaps there's a *really horrible* punishment in store for you. Maybe you'll be *forced* to endure extra science lessons with megatons of homework? And who *forces* you to obey these horrible laws anyway? Teachers? No.

Forces force you. Because forces force things to move. And a force can be anything from you flicking a pea, to the awesome gravity of a giant star. So the effects of forces can be an intergalactic explosion or the pea ending up in your teacher's ear hole. (This might cause an explosion too!)

But forces can have fascinating fatal effects. Like crushing people, or making them sick, or pulling their heads off. (Getting forces wrong at school isn't usually quite as fatal – just a bit of en-forced detention from your teacher.)

7

So here's the real-life story of forces. It's a story involving fatal fortunes and horrible happenings. And it's all true. And who knows? Afterwards you might feel that forces have a fatal attraction for you, too. You might even force your teacher to take your science homework seriously. If you can just force yourself to read the next page now . . .

NASTY NEWTON

The prisoner was sick. In the madness of his fever he imagined the courtroom candles were fiery ghosts. Again and again he heard the sentence of the judges: "Death!" Then he fainted.

He awoke in darkness. Dragging himself upright he tried to explore the pitch black cell. His feet slithered on the slimy floor. Then he stumbled, his hands grabbing at empty air. He'd collapsed on the edge of a bottomless pit. One more step and he'd have dropped like a stone. Exhausted, the prisoner fell asleep. But when he awoke he found himself strapped to a low bench. Helpless, he peered upwards and gasped in horror.

A giant statue towered over him. The grotesque figure had a huge pendulum swinging from its hands. The pendulum swung to and fro with an evil hiss. It ended in a razor-sharp blade and each slow sweep brought the blade a little lower. A little closer. Hiss . . . hiss . . . HISSSSSS! Scores of huge rats stared hungrily from the shadows, waiting to feast on the prisoner's butchered corpse. The deadly hissing blade skimmed his bare chest . . .

DON'T PANIC! It's only a story – *The Pit and the Pendulum* was written in 1849 by the American author Edgar Alan Poe. But Poe's story has a fatal fascination for scientists. The nasty forms of death – the pit and the pendulum – involve forces. Falling into the pit under the influence of gravity; the pendulum's swing controlled by gravity and centripetal force (see page 106). (That's the force on the pendulum shaft that stops the swinging weight from pulling away from the rest of the machine.) These forces are fatal for the prisoner.

HORRIBLE HEALTH WARNING!

Forces aren't human. You can't reason with them or persuade them. They are physical forces of nature with the power to kill. Fatal forces. Once you fall foul of fatal forces you're FINISHED!

Postscript:

Oh – by the way you'll be pleased to know the prisoner escapes. How? By getting the rats to gnaw through his straps, of course. Bet you didn't think of that! Amazingly enough these forces had already been explained by a forceful scientific mega-star, the amazing Sir Isaac Newton.

Hall of fame: Sir Isaac Newton (1642–1727)

Nationality: British

Isaac Newton was born on Christmas Day. The doctor thought baby Isaac wouldn't live because he was so weak and small.

But Isaac survived. He soon became interested in science but his teachers didn't think he was especially brainy. In fact, Isaac was too busy performing experiments at home to work hard at school. (Don't try this excuse.) When young Isaac was 16 his mum asked him to run the family farm. But he proved to be a useless farmer. He spent all his time experimenting and allowed the sheep to guzzle their way through a cornfield.

So Isaac went to Cambridge University instead. At university he read every math book he could find. (Including the ones without pictures.) He wore scruffy clothes and was so absent-minded he often got lost on his way to supper. As far as Isaac was concerned supper was for wimps. Who needed supper when you could do lovely science calculations instead?

In 1665 a deadly plague struck London. Soon 7,000 people were dying every week and the authorities closed Cambridge University to stop the plague spreading. So Isaac went home. But instead of taking a holiday he did *extra homework*. Very strange. But what homework! He invented calculus – a mathematical system still used today to plan rocket trips – and he also discovered that light contains colours.

These vital discoveries were to influence math and physics for 300 years. Then Isaac made a *really* incredible breakthrough. It may have happened like this . . .

THE APPLE AND THE MOON
Woolsthorpe, England 1666
It was getting dark, but the skinny young man ran his fingers through his shoulder-length hair and carried on reading. Isaac Newton was sitting in the orchard trying to figure out how the moon went around the Earth. Suddenly a call rang out from the old farmhouse:

"Hmm," thought Isaac, "she always calls me half an hour *before* supper. It's a trick to get me in on time."

So he did nothing. If he had left the orchard when his mother called him the entire history of science would have been different. But just then something grabbed his attention.

It had been waiting for this moment. Waiting for months, silently. At first it was no larger than a tiny green bulge. But now it was bright red and the size of a man's fist. A living bubble of water and sugars with sweet juicy flesh and bitter seeds all wrapped in a waxy skin. An apple. The most famous apple in science.

"Isaac! Your supper's on the table and it's your favourite!"

"Coming, Mother!"

Isaac shivered as a cool breeze rustled the trees. Then he sighed and reluctantly closed his book. There was a silent snap. The slender stalk holding the apple to the tree gave way. Wrenched by an unseen force the apple hurtled downward. It tumbled through the rustling leaves and bounced gently on Isaac's brainy bonce.

What would you have done? Perhaps you'd have eaten your supper and forgotten the apple. But Isaac wasn't like that. He rubbed his head and looked at the moon. It shone like a bright silver coin in the evening sky.

"So why doesn't the moon fall, too?" he asked himself, as he absent-mindedly munched the famous apple.

For some strange reason Isaac remembered his school and the dreaded "bucket game." He hated the other kids for making him play. He remembered having to whirl a bucket of water around his head on a rope. It was hard work and Isaac was a thin little boy. But amazingly all the water had stayed in the bucket as if trapped by an unseen force.

"Maybe that's what keeps the moon in place," he murmured.

Then his mother shouted again: "Isaac, your supper's on the table and it's stone cold."

"I said I'm coming, Mother!"

As Isaac threw the apple away he wondered what would happen if it reached the moon. The most famous apple core in science disappeared. There was a muffled meow as it splatted on the cat.

Isaac had forgotten his supper. He was calculating how strong gravity would need to be to stop the apple sailing into space. Then he thought about how fast the moon has to move to prevent it crashing down to Earth.

Later a very annoyed Mrs Newton stood in the doorway shielding her candle from the cold night air.

"Isaac!" she yelled. "I've fed your supper to the cat. And I'm going to feed your breakfast to the pigs!"

There was no answer from the orchard. But Isaac was still out there. And still thinking hard.

TEST YOUR TEACHER

How much does your teacher really know about this famous scientist?

1 As a child what was Isaac Newton's favourite toy?
a) A chemistry set.
b) A toy windmill powered by a mouse in a wheel.
c) He hated toys. He preferred tricky math sums.

2 What did he buy on his first day at university?
a) A desk, ink and a notebook for extra homework.
b) New clothes and a ticket to the local fun fair.
c) A loaf of bread to eat.

3 How did Newton solve tricky scientific problems?
a) The answers came in a flash of inspiration when Newton was on the toilet.
b) By talking things over with scientific friends.
c) Worrying away at the problem day and night until he figured out the answer.

4 Newton became Professor of Mathematics at Cambridge, but no one attended his bum-numbingly boring lectures.

So what did he do?

a) Rounded up students and *forced* them to listen.

b) Carried on talking to an empty room.

c) Tried to make his lectures interesting with a few jokes and amusing stories.

5 Newton's dog, Diamond, knocked over a candle and years of hard work went up in flames. What did he do?

a) Drew his sword and killed the dog.

b) Re-wrote his work from memory.

c) Told the dog off and went on to study something new and experimental.

Answers: 1 b) He designed it himself. **2 a)**, **3 c)**, **4 b)**
Does your teacher have this problem? **5 b)**.
What your teacher's score means.
1-2 Your teacher's guessing.
3-4 Your teacher knows a bit but doesn't know everything. (Much like any other teacher.)
5 Hard luck. Your teacher's read this book.

NEWTON'S MOVING BOOK

Newton didn't publish his discoveries for twenty years. He was too busy with his mathematical work. But then at last, fearful others might grab the glory, Newton wrote a book about his ideas. He shut himself away for eighteen months and worked twenty hours a day.

Sometimes Newton's assistant reminded him that he'd missed supper.

"Have I?" Newton would murmur sleepily. Then he'd nibble at the food and go back to work.

Newton's book was called *The Philosophiae Naturalis Principia Mathematica* and it was the most brilliant science book ever written. In it he explained the whole universe in a way that made sense. (Well – it would have made sense if the book hadn't been in Latin and filled with mystifying math.) Newton described gravity and three crucial laws about forces and how things move. These laws show how squids squirt water backwards in order to move forwards. They explain what happens when distant stars blow up and why low-flying sparrow droppings splat on your head.

One way to imagine Newton's laws is to think of a really horrible morning. What d'you mean – every day's like that?

What the law says . . .
If left alone a motionless object doesn't move. A moving object carries on moving in a straight line at a constant speed as long as another force doesn't make it change course.

What the law means . . .

You stare wearily at your breakfast. Your cornflakes are motionless and they're going to stay that way until you summon up the energy to eat them. You clumsily knock your spoon and half your breakfast goes flying. A cornflake falls on your dad's head. The cornflake would have flown in the same direction forever but the force of gravity pulled it down.

CORNFLAKE WOULD TRAVEL IN A STRAIGHT LINE FOREVER IF IT WASN'T FOR THE FORCE OF GRAVITY (AND THE CEILING).

OOPS! SORRY, DAD!

DOWNWARD FORCE OF THE HAND CATAPULTS THE CORNFLAKE UPWARDS

NEWTON'S SECOND LAW

What the law says...
When a force is applied to an object it changes its momentum.
The force makes the object move in the same direction as the force, at a speed proportional to the strength of this force.

What the law means . . .

That's why the force of a hefty kick can send a soccer ball whizzing towards a goalie at a deadly speed.

NEWTON'S THIRD LAW

What the law says...
When an object exerts a force on another object the second object will push back just as hard.

What the law means . . .

You're late and you're jogging to school. But you're still not properly awake. You slam into a lamppost. And the lamppost wallops you back! It's true – this really does happen.

***

Bet you never knew!

When Newton's apple hit the ground the Earth bumped against the apple. That's what Newton's Third Law says: things always push back with equal force. But the Earth moved such a tiny distance no one noticed. Oddly enough a unit of force was later named the "Newton" in the scientist's honour. And the weight produced by one Newton is roughly the same as . . . an apple. But Newton was no ordinary genius. He had a nasty side, too.

NEWTON'S NASTY NATURE

1 When Newton was three years old his mum remarried. Isaac hated his stepfather and often thought of killing him. He didn't, of course, but he was pleased when the stepfather died.

2 At school Newton had no friends until he thumped the school bully with great force. Newton was smaller than his opponent but his courage helped win the fight. After this nasty incident Newton became popular.

3 Newton disliked women and never married. He hated his friend John Locke's attempts to introduce him to ladies. Later Newton wrote to Locke:

when ... (a woman) told me you were sickly and would not live, I answered t'were better you were dead

THANKS A LOT!

But that didn't stop Newton from generously allowing his niece Catherine to do his cooking and cleaning.

4 Newton was a miserable man. He had no hobbies apart from work. He rarely laughed and he called poetry:

A KIND OF INGENIOUS NONSENSE

5 In 1686 Newton fell out with scientist Robert Hooke (1635–1703). Hooke unjustly accused Newton of pinching *his* ideas on gravity. In a letter Newton called Hooke "a pretender and a grasper" and refused to talk to him.

6 After writing the *Principia* Newton had a nasty turn. He went mad for two years and did no scientific research. Some historians reckon Newton was a bit depressed but others say he was poisoned by the mercury he used for chemistry experiments.

7 When he got better Newton was appointed Warden of the Royal Mint and reformed Britain's coinage. It was said that nasty Newton enjoyed catching forgers and arranging especially nasty executions for them.

I WILL NOW DEMONSTRATE ANOTHER OF THE FATAL FORCES...

8 German Gottfried Leibniz (1646–1716) claimed he invented calculus. Newton accused Leibniz of pinching his idea. But in fact Leibniz had made the discovery independently at the same time as Newton. (And it was Leibniz who actually coined the word "calculus" – Newton called it "fluxions" – which sounds like the effects of a nasty tummy bug.)

9 Newton came to a horrible end. He moved to the country to improve his health. But a few weeks later he fell sick and died of a stone in his bladder. By then, however, he was a nasty-tempered old man of 84, but still a great genius.

NEWTON IN HIS OWN WORDS

Like many geniuses Newton was hard to understand. Here's what he said about himself:

Note: Newton didn't mean human pyramids. The giants he referred to were earlier scientists who inspired him. He also said:

Note: Newton meant that he'd learnt enough to realize there was more to learn. He was right. He'd only scratched the surface. There are loads more fatally fascinating facts about forces. You'll find them in the next chapter.

FORCEFUL FACTS

Forces are *everywhere*. You can't do much without bumping into them. But hopefully not with a fatal *CRUNCH*. Oddly enough, though, before Newton, people knew very little about how forces worked.

MIXED-UP MOTION THEORIES

A scientist will tell you that a force is something that affects the movement or shape of an object or person. Sounds fairly vague. But before Newton, scientific theories were even more mixed-up. One of the first people to write about forces was a Greek genius called Aristotle.

Hall of fame: Aristotle (384–322 BC)
Nationality: Greek

Aristotle was a doctor's son. His parents died when he was a child and as a young man he blew their money on wild parties. But when he was seventeen years old Aristotle had a sudden change of heart and sent himself back to school.

WEIRD! I SUDDENLY FEEL LIKE DOING LOADS OF HOMEWORK!

He went to study under the brainy philosopher called Plato in the Academy at Athens. Aristotle liked it there so much that he stayed for the next twenty years as a pupil and then as a teacher.

Aristotle travelled for four years and eventually moved to Macedonia where his old mate Philip happened to be king. Phil asked Aristotle to teach his boy, Alexander. Aristotle must have done a good job because young Alexander became Alexander the Great and conquered a great chunk of Asia. By the time Aristotle died (of acute indigestion) he had written about everything from politics to how grasshoppers chirp. And he even had a few things to say about forces.

MYSTERY MOTIONS

Here's how Aristotle explained forces:

27

Wrong, wrong and wrong again. But for 2,000 years everyone thought Aristotle's wacko ideas were RIGHT. Eventually Newton used math to prove Aristotle WRONG. So nowadays we've got forces figured out. As a scientist might say, "Learning about forces is as easy as riding a bike." Oh, yeah? Riding a bike is LOADS harder and just to prove it we've asked a scientist to try.

Scientific cycling in ten easy lessons

THE SMALL PRINT:
IT'S NOT OUR FAULT IF YOU END
UP IN HOSPITAL — OK?

LESSON 1: WOBBLY BALANCE

Remember learning to ride a bike? Tough, wasn't it? Inside the scientist's ears are fluid-filled spaces, called semi-circular canals. (Teachers have a larger air-filled space where their brains should be. Ha, ha.) These canals help her balance on two wheels. As the liquid sloshes around, sensors tell her brain whether she's still upright. Her brilliant brain also notices the force of gravity, her speed, the slope and wind direction. Yep – all at the same time.

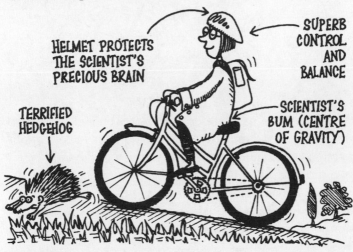

HELMET PROTECTS
THE SCIENTIST'S
PRECIOUS BRAIN

SUPERB
CONTROL
AND
BALANCE

TERRIFIED
HEDGEHOG

SCIENTIST'S
BUM (CENTRE
OF GRAVITY)

It helps her balance if her science books, sandwiches, etc. aren't draped over one handlebar. Ideally her bum is the centre of gravity – the point around which everything else is sensibly balanced.

LESSON 2: EFFORTLESS INERTIA

Inertia means that things at rest tend to stay put. That's why it takes more energy to start cycling than to keep going. But our scientist has got to start somewhere. So she gets pedalling and once she's moving it's easier to carry on. Inertia helps her keep going in a straight line. But she still needs a bit more peddling and puffing. Phew!

OH DEAR!
THE HILL SEEMS
TO HAVE GOT
A BIT STEEPER

PUFF!
GASP!

HILLS REQUIRE
MORE ENERGY

SCIENTIST HAS
TO PUSH DOWN
HARDER ON
THE PEDALS

LESSON 3: MASS-IVE MOMENTUM

Momentum is a measure of the scientist's ability to keep going. And her momentum depends on her mass. If your reaction to this statement is to say "yer wot?", you'd better read the next bit. Mass means how much there is of the scientist – everything in her body, her clothes and even what she had for breakfast. Her mass, her bike's mass and her speed combine to produce her momentum. Wheee!

WHEEEE

WHOOSH

NO NEED
TO PEDAL

NOT
AGAIN!

LESSON 4: MIXED-UP MOMENTUM

Oops! She's knocked the school bully flying. Scientists would say she's "transferred momentum" to the bully and call this "conserving momentum." The posh scientific word for speed in one direction is "velocity." So she'd better pedal at quite a velocity in order to conserve her life!

TRANSFER OF MOMENTUM TAKES PLACE HERE

BULLY LANDS SOMEWHERE OVER HERE

BAD

Uh-oh, the bully's heading towards her on a skateboard. THEY'RE GOING TO CRASH! As they crash the two momentums cancel each other. So they both grind to a halt. Result = TROUBLE!!!

LESSON 5: GALLOPING GRAVITY

Velocity is greater when cycling downhill. Gravity tries to pull the scientist to the centre of the Earth. And the bottom of the slope is a bit nearer the centre of the planet than the top. This explains why, if she loses her balance, it's easier to fall off her bike than stay on. By the way, if she did make it right through to the Earth's centre, there would be no gravity and she would float around being roasted in the fiery heat. Not nice! Tired yet? Our scientist is. She's run out of kinetic energy. That's the posh scientific name for the energy she uses when moving. Oh well – we'll give her a few minutes to recover and then we'll put her back to work.

LESSON 6: AWKWARD ACCELERATION AND DRAG

For the scientist the word "acceleration" means changing speed or direction. So even when she slows down, she calls it "acceleration." But when she accelerates down a hill she feels the wind whistling up her nostrils (and everywhere else), and trying to slow her. This force is called "drag." If it's particularly windy it'll "drag" her off her bike – the result could be fatal.

WIND BLOWS AGAINST THE SCIENTIST AND CAUSES "DRAG" WHICH SLOWS HER DOWN

CROUCHING DOWN REDUCES THE DRAG AND HELPS HER TO GO FASTER!

LESSON 7: CURIOUS CORNERING

As the scientist rounds the corner, centripetal (sen-tri-puh-tul) force pulls her bike into the corner. But her body's momentum tries to make her move in a straight line (Newton's First Law) and she *feels* as if a force is throwing her outwards. In fact there is no such force – it's all in the scientist's imagination!

SCIENTIST LEANS THIS WAY →

TO COUNTER-BALANCE HER MOMENTUM ←

LESSON 8: GRINDING GEARS

The gears on the scientist's bike help her cycle uphill. The gears allow her to pedal quicker but with less force. This means she can cycle up the slope without getting puffed out. Yep – gears are great. As a scientist would say, "They're a great way of transferring forces."

LESSON 9: FURIOUS FRICTION

The force of friction slows moving objects. It happens when a moving object touches another object. The scientist's tires grip the road and provide this force. This helps her control the bike and avoid fatal collisions. Lack of friction makes cycling on ice a slippery experience. And performing wheelies on the local rink is definitely out.

When she wants to slow down or stop the rubber brakes grip her wheels and friction stops her bike. Hopefully. If she brakes too hard, her momentum throws her forward, and she performs spectacular but possibly fatal handlebar acrobatics.

LESSON 10: VICIOUS VIBRATIONS

When the scientist rides her bike along a bumpy path she may feel a few vibrations. These are shock waves carrying the force of impact from the tires. Her tires and saddle springs are designed to soak up some vibrations. But that doesn't stop her body vibrating, her muscles twitching and her eyeballs bouncing slightly in their sockets.

FREAKY PHYSICISTS

Scientists who study forces are called physicists (fizz-i-sists). They also explore motion, probe what things are made of and try to figure out how the universe works. A typical physicist is slightly scruffy and enjoys tinkering with things. A physics lab is rather untidy and full of bits and pieces that have been salvaged in order to build a freaky machine.

FATAL EXPRESSIONS

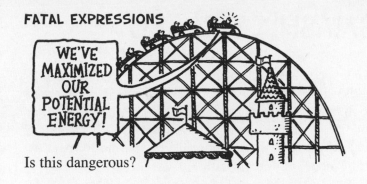

WE'VE MAXIMIZED OUR POTENTIAL ENERGY!

Is this dangerous?

Answer: Just a bit. By the time the roller-coaster gets to the top of the slope it has built up a lot of energy to make it zoom downhill really fast. HOLD ON TO YOUR LUNCH!

Bet you never knew!

Physicists use two strange words in connection with forces – "energy" and "work." Well, hopefully they don't sound too strange to you. But we're not talking about summoning up the energy to do homework or wash the dishes here. No way.

Physicists say "work" when they want to explain what happens when a force causes an object to move a distance. According to them writing your math homework is "work" but reckoning up the answers in your head isn't. Energy is the ability to do work. Sounds sensible – after all you need energy to work. Don't you?

Just thinking about energy and work is pretty exhausting, so why don't you take a little rest? Yeah – put your feet up. Get your breath back for the next chapter. You'll need it 'cos it's about speed and crashes! Fasten your safety belt.

SMASHING SPEED

Some people think speed is smashing. Others don't. Early railways scared some people because they reckoned no human could go faster than 32 km per hour (20 mph) and live. Well, they can, of course. But one thing's certain – the faster you go the more likely you are to meet up with some fatal forces. Gulp!

TEST YOUR TEACHER
Is your teacher quick-witted? Smile sweetly and ask:

WHAT WAS THE FASTEST SPEED ATTAINED ON A BICYCLE DURING THE NINETEENTH CENTURY?

(Note the subtle wording – your teacher probably thinks you're talking about pedalling – but she'd be wrong.)

Your teacher will probably say something like, "50 km per hour" (31 mph) – hopelessly wrong. At this point you can say, "No, I think you're wrong. In 1899 Mr C.M. Murphy smashed the record. He tied his bike to the back of a train and travelled 1.6 km in a minute." *Don't* try this at home.

QUICK QUIZ

1 Super speedy

See if you can put these three objects in order of speed, starting with the fastest.

a) A bullet from a high-powered rifle.

b) The planet Mercury moving through space.

c) Three astronauts aboard the Apollo 10 spacecraft in 1969.

2 Fairly speedy

Which of these three objects do you think is the fastest?

a) A chameleon's tongue as it grabs a juicy fly.

b) A message sent along one of your nerves.

c) A person falling from the top of a 99.4-metre-high building.

3 Slow and sluggish

Can you put these three objects in order of speed starting with thc fastest?

a) Your fingernails growing.

b) Bamboo plants growing.

c) The Atlantic Ocean getting wider.

Answers: 1 b) 172,248 km per hour (107,030 mph) When it comes to orbiting the sun, Mercury is the speediest planet in the solar system. **c)** 39,897 km per hour (24,791 mph) Feeling a teensy bit space sick? **a)** 3,302 km per hour (2,052 mph). That's too fast to see. The bullet travels faster than sound so a person could be shot before they heard the gun firing. Doesn't sound fair somehow.

2 b) 483 km per hour (300 mph). **c)** 141 km per hour (80 mph). This was the speed achieved by stuntman Dan Koko in 1984 as he leapt off the Las Vegas World Hotel. Lucky for Dan he smashed into an air cushion rather than the pavement. **a)** 80.5 km per hour (50 mph). Then it's bye-bye fly.

3 b) 3 cm an hour. If your fingernails grew any faster than this, you'd have problems. **c)** 0.0006 cm an hour. The Atlantic Ocean is getting wider due to the movements of enormous slabs of rock deep beneath the Earth's surface. **a)** 0.00028 cm an hour. Any faster than this and it could be fatal.

Bet you never knew!
You'd move faster if your shape allowed the air to flow around you rather than bumping into you. This kind of shape is called "aerodynamic" and it cuts down on drag. A bullet with its pointed head is an aerodynamic shape but a human head isn't. If it was we'd all have pointy heads. Record-smashing speed cyclists wear pointed helmets instead. And more speed means more momentum. Smashing!

NAME: Momentum

THE BASIC FACTS: Momentum keeps you moving. That way you don't smash Newton's First Law. (That's the one about going in a straight line unless something stops you.)

THE HORRIBLE DETAILS: Momentum makes your stomach jump when you go over the top on a roller coaster.

ARGHHHH!

The momentum of your half-digested food carries on up. If it comes up too far it could be fatally embarrassing!

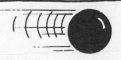

CHATTER TREMBLE

MURDEROUS MOMENTUM FACTS

1 In 1871 showman John Holtum tried to catch a flying cannonball *with his bare hands*. It wasn't fired from a real cannon, of course. Holtum used a specially built gun that fired a slow-moving ball. But even so he nearly lost a finger. The stunt proved very popular and John bravely practised until he'd perfected the trick. He should have changed his name to "Halt-em."

2 In nineteenth-century America railways were rarely fenced off and brainless buffalo often blundered onto the tracks. To tackle this menace, by the 1860s trains were fitted with wedge-shaped "cow catchers." The idea was that the train's momentum would scoop the buffalo out of harm's way.

3 In Canada moose cause fatal road accidents. When hit by a car, the momentum of the vehicle flips the moose over. So the loose moose lands on the car roof. Its weight crushes both the car and its driver. Perhaps the cars should be fitted with "moose catchers."

IDLE INERTIA
Physicists use the word inertia to describe how things stay the same. Motionless things stay idle and moving things carry on until another force gets in the way. That's Newton's First Law again.

Dare you discover . . . the inertia of an egg?
You will need:
A plate
A raw egg
A hard-boiled egg

What you do:

1 Gently spin the raw egg on the plate.

2 To stop the egg touch it with your finger.

3 Gently lift your finger up.

4 Now repeat steps 1–3 with the hard-boiled egg.

What did you notice?

a) When you lifted your finger the hard-boiled egg continued to spin.

b) When you lifted your finger the raw egg continued to spin.

c) When you lifted your finger the raw egg spun and the hard-boiled egg rocked from end-to-end.

WHOOPS

DON'T PUSH
DOWN
TOO HARD

about smashing things . . .

Answer: b) When you stopped the raw egg, inertia kept the egg white inside spinning. And this started the entire egg spinning again when you lifted your finger. The inside of the hard-boiled egg is hard, of course, so the white doesn't have its own inertia.

Important note: The egg should spin on the plate. Not spin through the air and smash on the floor. If this happens you'll be force-fed an omelette. And talking

A SMASHING TEST

Car designers spend fortunes building new cars. And then they smash them up. This may sound stupid, but they need to test the car's structural design and materials under crash conditions to find the best ways to ensure that the driver and passengers are as well protected as possible. These days most smashes happen on a computer screen. The engineers peer at a simulation of crashes at various speeds. They can even slow down the movement to one image every two milliseconds – that's far slower than a TV action replay.

But afterwards the engineers need real-life tests to check their findings. And this is when the poor old dummies get wheeled in to show the effects of the crash on real people. Of course, dummies don't have brains – that's why they're dummies. But they do have a smashing time.

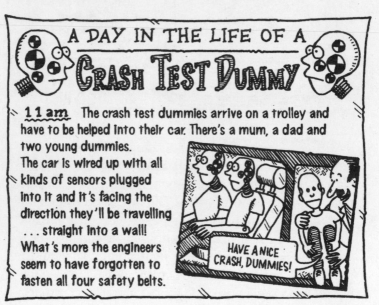

A DAY IN THE LIFE OF A CRASH TEST DUMMY

11 am The crash test dummies arrive on a trolley and have to be helped into their car. There's a mum, a dad and two young dummies.

The car is wired up with all kinds of sensors plugged into it and it's facing the direction they'll be travelling ... straight into a wall! What's more the engineers seem to have forgotten to fasten all four safety belts.

HAVE A NICE CRASH, DUMMIES!

11.02 am The engineers crouch behind steel barriers to protect themselves from the impact of the crash, and it turns out they *deliberately* forgot about the safety belts. Steel cables at the front of the car catapult it forward at speed. CRAACK! the car hits the wall. The dummies crash through the windshield. The front of the car is completely smashed in.

12.00 noon
The dummies are cut free from the wreckage. They're a little bit battered but they've survived to crash another day. They're pretty tough dummies.

1.00 pm
The engineers stop for a sandwich. The dummies aren't all that hungry.

SUIT YOURSELF!

2.00 pm Telly time! The dummies have become movie stars, but they don't even know it. As the dummies are wheeled away the engineers settle themselves in front of a screen to watch an action replay of the crash on video.

You can see how Newton's First Law affects the dummies. That's the law about things continuing to move in a straight line. When the car stops, the inertia of the dummies forces

them to carry on moving – straight through the windshield. So the force of the wall hitting the car is transferred to the poor old dummies. You can see why seat belts are lifesavers. You'd be a real dummy not to wear one.

5.00 pm The engineers set up tomorrow's test. This time the dummies will be trapped in a car as it rolls over in a crash. But that's just another smashing day in the life of the crash test dummies.
A dummy's life is full of hard knocks.

Safety first

As a result of this testing, engineers have come up with a few ingenious devices to help reduce the impact of a car crash on passengers:

SCIENTIST'S CAR

WUMPFF!

Collapsible steering wheel. If the air bag fails, the steering wheel collapses rather than spearing the driver in the chest.

Seat belts soak up the force that throws the body forward.

Airbags If a driver is thrown forward onto the steering wheel of most modern cars, the bag inflates for a nice soft landing.

FORCE 1

Crumple zones (found in some new cars). When the car crashes, part of the front of the car is designed to crumple up and soak up some of the shock.

Side-impact bars (found in some new cars). Strengthens the doors so they won't get smashed in if another car whacks into them.

SMASHING SOUND SPEEDS

Fatal though they often are, the forces in a car crash are nothing compared to those in really high-speed accidents like an air crash. Or the horrible effects of falling out of an airplane at high speed. The effects of high speeds were studied by Austrian physicist Ernst Mach (1838–1916). Mach found that it's hard to travel faster than the speed of sound – 1,220 km per hour (760 mph). (By the way, the speed of sound is the speed at which sounds travel through the air.)

Here's why it was so difficult. All aircraft push air in front of them. But a plane flying at the speed of sound smashes into this air before it can escape. This makes for a violently bumpy ride that can shake the plane to pieces (not to mention your insides). In the 1940s several pilots died trying to smash the sound barrier. But in 1947 American pilot Charles E. Yeager broke the barrier in a rocket-powered plane. It was known to be dangerous to fly really, really fast, but at this time no one knew what hitting the air at these speeds would do to an unprotected body. Could it be fatal?

FLY FOR YOUR LIFE

February 26, 1955, California, USA

At 9:30 am precisely, ace test pilot George Franklin Smith picked up his washing. He turned left out of the launderette and walked slap bang into the worst day of his life.

He should have known better. How many people volunteer to work on a Saturday? But he had nothing better to do than finish a report. And of course when he got to work someone offered him a test flight in a gleaming brand-new F-100 Super Sabre jet. This was a new type of jet plane capable of flying faster than sound.

George grinned. He loved test flying the powerful planes. In his laid-back way he replied:

YEAH, SURE I'LL TAKE HER UP. WON'T TAKE MORE THAN FORTY-FIVE MINUTES OR SO.

It wasn't worth putting on a protective suit.

As George took off he noticed the controls were a bit stiff. But there seemed nothing to worry about – the pre-flight checks had been just fine. He chatted happily to a pilot friend over the intercom.

Minutes later he broke the sound barrier. Then the plane nosed down and the controls jammed. The jet was diving to destruction at supersonic speed.

As his speed increased George yelled: "Controls locked – I'm going straight down!"

His friend's voice exploded in the headphones. "Bail out, George! Get out of there!" He had seconds to escape or die.

About 2,100 metres below the blue sea glittered in the sunshine.

George wrenched the armrest and jettisoned the jet's Perspex canopy. A tearing gale filled the cockpit. At this speed the violent force of the air pinned him down. He painfully stretched out his hand. His fingertips brushed the ejector seat handle. There was no time. No time to think of the danger. *Every* pilot who had bailed out at supersonic speeds had been killed.

George's straining fingers clutched the handle. *KERBAAAM!* A powerful explosion tore him from the cockpit. He hit a wall of air. The world and the sky tumbled crazily. In a few seconds his shoes and socks, his watch and helmet were torn away. He was bleeding heavily and very, very scared.

His falling body felt like a feather. "A falling body" he thought vaguely, "has no weight – it's . . . something to do with gravity." There was a crack and a sharp jerk as the parachute opened, its canopy trapping and slowing the air as it rushed past. Then George felt himself slip into darkness. He felt no pain as his body slammed into the sea and began to sink.

"Hey, give me a hand!" shouted the fisherman to his friend as he hauled the heavy body from the water.

The other man looked doubtful. "There's no point – I think the pilot's dead."

But George Smith was still alive. Just . . .

The Air Force took a month to scoop up all the mangled pieces of George's plane from the sea bed 1.6 km from the shore. The wreckage filled fifty barrels and still no one knew what had caused the crash.

But scientists now had a chance to study the effect of extreme forces . . . on poor George's half-dead body.

Here's what they found out:

1 As George ejected from the plane his speed boosted the effects of gravity. What we call "weight" depends on the strength of the gravity affecting our bodies. So every part of the pilot's body became 40 times heavier. You may have felt this yourself. It's that weird feeling of being stuck to your seat as you climb a roller coaster. Only George was moving much faster so this effect was almost fatal.

2 Even his blood became heavier for a few moments. Heavy blood squirted from his heavy blood vessels. This caused a mass of bruises to appear on his body. He was so bruised that his head swelled up like a purple football.

3 George's eyelids bled after fluttering violently in the howling wind as he fell fast.

In all George spent seven months in hospital. But he made a full recovery and went back to flying. He was the luckiest pilot in the world. Of course, every pilot's worst nightmare is to fall out of the sky. Because falling – under the influence of gravity – can be fatal. So if you want to survive the next chapter you'd better hang on tight. And DON'T FORGET YOUR PARACHUTE!

GRUESOME GRAVITY

What goes up must come down. This old saying is true as long as you're not in outer space where things float around all the time and don't "come down." Why? Because there's no gravity in space to bring you down to Earth. So what is this unearthly force? Read on for the full and gruesome details.

Fatal forces fact file

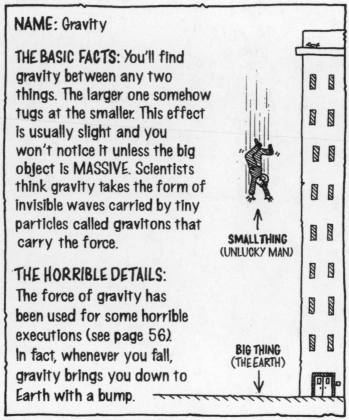

NAME: Gravity

THE BASIC FACTS: You'll find gravity between any two things. The larger one somehow tugs at the smaller. This effect is usually slight and you won't notice it unless the big object is MASSIVE. Scientists think gravity takes the form of invisible waves carried by tiny particles called gravitons that carry the force.

SMALL THING (UNLUCKY MAN)

THE HORRIBLE DETAILS: The force of gravity has been used for some horrible executions (see page 56). In fact, whenever you fall, gravity brings you down to Earth with a bump.

BIG THING (THE EARTH)

TERMINAL VELOCITY

How's this for a thrill? You go for a flight in a plane up to, say, 6,100 metres and then you jump out. And you don't use a parachute. Well – not until you've fallen halfway to the ground under the influence of gravity. Is this completely crazy? No, it's a popular sport called free-fall parachuting. If you don't mind heights and enjoy a bit of danger you'll love this. If not, you'd better put on a blindfold before you read this next bit.

HOW TO BE A FREE-FALL PARACHUTIST IN ONE QUICK LESSON

1 Try not to look at the ground. Jump out of the plane.
2 Check your parachute is strapped securely to your back. (Come to think of it, that should have been Step One.)

3 Start tumbling. That's not something you've got to do – it's something that will happen to you anyway. You'll find your sense of balance can't help you stay upright. You'll feel sick. Try not to panic at this stage.

4 For 15 seconds you fall faster and faster. Every second you fall 9.8 metres faster until you hit – 50 metres a second (100–150 mph). That's the maximum speed you can fall. It's called terminal velocity. Gulp! It's horrible feeling there's nothing under you except empty air, but some people can't get enough of it.

5 Good news. You won't fall any faster because the air slows you down – this force is known as drag.

6 Here's your chance to practise your free-fall parachuting technique. Try to fall face downwards. Spread your arms and legs and stick your stomach out. You'll find your body curves forwards and your arms and legs are pushed backwards.

This makes a larger area for the drag to act upon. So you don't fall quite so fast. Flying squirrels and sky-diving cats do this in mid-air.

7 One minute later. Had fun? Good. You're going to hit the ground in 25 seconds. Better pull your parachute rip cord now or you'll really fall foul of gravity. And make a rather deep hole in the ground.

8 As you land make sure you drop down to a squatting position. Bending your knees soaks up some force as you hit the ground. Enjoyed it? Great – you'll be falling over yourself to make another jump.

If you don't happen to have a parachute things can get a teensy bit more difficult. In 1944 Flight-Sergeant Nicholas Alkemade was in desperate danger 5,500 metres above Germany. His plane was on fire and his parachute was burnt to a cinder. He jumped and fully expected to die. But he was lucky. He fell on top of a tree and then onto a deep bank of snow and as a result much of the force of his fall was soaked up. Alkemade survived to tell his remarkable story and he didn't even break any bones!

MORE GRUESOME GRAVITY

In the past gravity was used to make executions more efficient. During a hanging the victim dropped through a trapdoor and gravity acting on the rope broke the victim's neck. If the drop was too far the force yanked their head off too. Gruesome!

Another gruesome method of execution was the guillotine. This featured a 30.4 kg weight attached to a sharp blade. The force powering the gruesome blade as it fell was gravity. In the 1790s working model guillotines were popular children's toys. Their parents must have been off their heads.

In England in the seventeenth century criminals who refused to plead guilty or not guilty at their trials were crushed to death under heavy weights. Once again it was gravity doing the damage. You may be interested to know that a louse can withstand a force of 500,000 times its own weight. Unfortunately for the criminals, humans scrunch more easily.

Now for something a bit less fatal. Hopefully. You'd think that lying on a bed of nails would turn you into a gruesome human pin cushion. Surely gravity pins you to those nasty nails? Not necessarily. You can press down with a force of 450 g on a nail without harm. (Don't try proving this at home – nails are usually crawling with disgusting germs.) So 400 nails can support a huge 182 kg man for a comfortable night's sleep. Bet that's a weight off your mind.

FATAL EXPRESSIONS

Answer: No. He's got a weight problem. Scientists say "mass" instead of weight because weight is just a measure of how strongly gravity is pulling you towards the Earth. Some Americans measure mass using a unit called the "slug." The overweight scientist weighs about ten slugs – 145 kg. Mind you, scientists use kilograms instead of slugs. The moon's gravity is weaker than Earth's, so a human only weighs $\frac{1}{6}$ as much there.

TEST YOUR TEACHER

Your teacher's bound to fall down on this really tricky question. Smile sweetly and say:

EXCUSE ME, IS IT TRUE THAT GRAVITY CAN HELP YOU LOSE WEIGHT?

Answer: Yes – but you'd have to be in an elevator with a set of scales to prove it. If one day the elevator cable snaps, quickly leap on the scales. In the few seconds you take to hurtle to the ground you're weightless! Weight is just a measure of gravity's pull. But when you fall you're not resisting gravity and you're weightless! You can blame Galileo for all this, he was the first person to discover how the force works.

Hall of fame: Galileo Galilei (1564–1642)
Nationality: Italian

Young Galileo wanted to study math (strange boy), but his dad forced him to learn medicine instead. Doctors got more pay than mathematicians. But sneaky Galileo secretly studied sums until his dad gave up on him. When he was twenty-five, Galileo became a math professor at Pisa University. Then he got interested in gravity and performed amazing experiments to measure the force. Here's what his notebooks may have looked like.

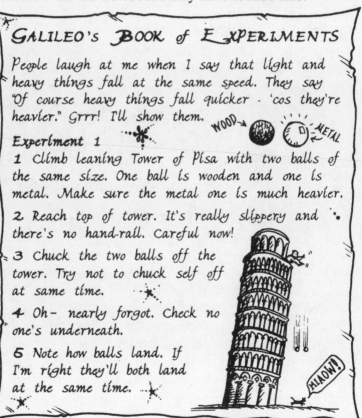

GALILEO'S BOOK of EXPERIMENTS

People laugh at me when I say that light and heavy things fall at the same speed. They say "Of course heavy things fall quicker - 'cos they're heavier." Grrr! I'll show them.

WOOD→   ←METAL

Experiment 1

1 Climb leaning Tower of Pisa with two balls of the same size. One ball is wooden and one is metal. Make sure the metal one is much heavier.

2 Reach top of tower. It's really slippery and there's no hand-rail. Careful now!

3 Chuck the two balls off the tower. Try not to chuck self off at same time.

4 Oh - nearly forgot. Check no one's underneath.

5 Note how balls land. If I'm right they'll both land at the same time.

MIAOW!

ME

People still don't believe me.
Huh - this'll teach them a lesson.

Experiment 2

1 Get a wooden board with a little wooden gully on it. Line it with some nice shiny parchment made from animal skin with the fat scraped off.

USE SKIN FROM CAT KILLED IN EXPERIMENT 1

2 Raise the gully on a slope and roll a bronze ball down it. (If you don't have a bronze ball any other metal will do.)

3 Be sure to precisely measure the time taken for the ball to roll to the bottom of the slope. OOPS - silly me, I was about to forget, no one's invented an accurate clock yet. Better use pulse to time ball's speed. Mustn't get too excited, or my pulse will be racing. Better repeat the test a few times to make sure.

3, 4, 5, 6, 7, ...

RUMBLE RUMBLE

4 I believe gravity makes things accelerate at the same speed. If I'm right balls of different weights will roll at the same speed too.

Notes:

1 Galileo was proved right in both experiments.
2 It should be pointed out that boring old historians reckon there's no proof Galileo performed the first experiment. Huh – why spoil a good story?

GALILEO'S GENIUS

There's no doubt Galileo was a genius. He invented the thermometer, a pendulum driven clock and an amazing compass that you could use to work out the purity of metals. He even discovered that cannonballs fall in a curved path. They move forwards at a constant speed and downwards at an increasing speed under the influence of gravity. This fatal discovery helped gunners fire more accurately and kill more people.

Could you think like Galileo? Now's your chance to find out.

BURNING AMBITION QUIZ

1 You are Galileo. You look through the newly invented telescope and see planets orbiting the sun. (As Newton later proved, gravity stops them wandering off into space.) But there's one teeny little problem. Important people in the Catholic Church claim planets go around the Earth. They're all-powerful in Italy, and they don't want a smarty-pants scientist proving them wrong. You realize you'd be wise to get the backing of these people. What do you do?

a) Start a reasoned debate.

b) Get them to look through your telescope.

c) Shout at them until they admit you're right.

LISTEN, YOU OLD FOOL, THE POTATO GOES ROUND THE BOILED EGG — NOT THE OTHER WAY ROUND!

2 You reckon the Church's experts that you talked to are friendly. They aren't. Your enemies falsely accuse you of being anti-Church. What do you do?

a) Go into hiding.

b) Write a book making fun of your enemies.

c) Set the record straight in a public statement.

3 In 1623 you have a stroke of luck. An old pal of yours is elected Pope. You drop in for a chat. He allows you to write a book so long as it doesn't support your views. What's in the book?

a) Support for your views and amusing abuse of your enemies.

b) A balanced survey of the different opinions that doesn't come to any conclusions.

c) A cleverly written argument which seems to back the traditional view whilst actually making it look stupid.

4 Your book is a best-seller but the Pope is chewing the carpet. You're accused of heresy and put on trial before the dreaded Inquisition. Your enemies forge a letter that claims the Church had banned you from teaching your views. If you're found guilty you could be tied to a stake and burnt alive. What do you do?

a) Proudly insist you were right.

b) Quietly remind the Pope that you're his friend.

c) Crack a joke about liking your "stake" well done.

5 In a bid to scare you, the Inquisition shows you the torture chamber that is used to extract confessions. You see the rack, the thumbscrews and the red hot pincers. What do you say?

a) OK, where's the confession – I'll sign anything . . . Oh dear, I can't sign that, it's not grovelling enough.

b) The truth is the truth. I scorn your puny instruments of torture and laugh in the face of danger.

c) Can I have twenty years to think about it, please?

WOBBLY BALANCE

Everything has a centre of gravity. Imagine a tightrope walker.

65

Her centre of balance is the point inside her body where gravity is pulling most strongly. If this crucial point is supported underneath and the performer's weight is evenly balanced around it she's OK. If not there'll be a gloopy mess on the pavement. Yet some balancing acts seem impossible.

WOBBLY BALANCING QUIZ

See if you can guess which of these incredible balancing acts are true and which are false.

1 In 1553 a Dutch acrobat balanced on one foot on the weather vane of St Paul's Cathedral, London waving a 4.6-metre streamer. And he didn't fall off.
TRUE/FALSE

2 In 1859 French tightrope walker Jean Blondin (1824–1897) walked across the raging Niagara Falls, 50 metres in the air. And he was wearing a blindfold.
TRUE/FALSE
3 In 1773 Dutch acrobat Leopold van Trump juggled ten tomatoes whilst balancing on a tightrope 30 metres in the air. If he had fallen he might have invented ketchup.
TRUE/FALSE

4 In 1842 a Miss Cooke wowed London circus goers when she sat at a table and drank a glass of wine. Boring? Not really. Everything was balanced on a high wire.
TRUE/FALSE

5 In 1995 Aleksandr Bendikov of Belarus balanced a pyramid made of 880 coins. The coin pyramid was upside down and balanced on top of the edge of a single coin. Luckily, no one needed change for the bus.
TRUE/FALSE

6 In 2007 American Bryan Berg built a house of cards that was 7.86 metres tall – taller than most 2-storey homes!
TRUE/FALSE

7 In 1990 Brazilian Leandro Henrique Basseto cycled on one wheel of his bicycle for 100 minutes.
TRUE/FALSE

Yes, it's amazing what incredible death-defying, gravity-defying, balancing acts people can do just as long as the force of gravity is exactly balanced. But getting it right on the high-wire certainly puts you under pressure. And oddly enough, the next chapter is about pressure too. The kind of pressure that can fatally crush a human being. Ouch!

I'VE BEEN UNDER A LOT OF PRESSURE RECENTLY

UNDER PRESSURE

Air and water are common enough on Earth but they contain vital chemicals – in fact we couldn't live without them. But if they're under pressure it's hard to live with them. And they can easily prove fatal.

Fatal forces fact file

NAME: Air and water pressure

THE BASIC FACTS: When tiny bits of air and water (molecules) are pushed aside by an object they push back. That's why when you get into a deep bath you can feel the water pushing against your body. It's what is called water pressure.

THE HORRIBLE DETAILS: The deeper you go the more water there is above you. This means more pressure. Divers breathe air that's also under pressure to stop their lungs getting squashed.

THIS SUBMARINE'S AMAZING – IT EVEN HAS A SHOWER IN IT...

ACTUALLY, THAT'S CALLED A LEAK, CAPTAIN

One of the first people to study air pressure was French physicist Blaise Pascal.

Hall of fame: Blaise Pascal (1623–1662)
Nationality: French

Blaise Pascal had no sense of humour. Not surprising really, he suffered all his life from violent indigestion so he didn't have the stomach for too many jokes. But that didn't stop brainy Blaise from making some amazing discoveries. At the age of 19 he built a machine to help his tax collector dad count up the loot. And in 1646 he invented a barometer – a machine that measures air pressure. High air pressure pushes a column of mercury upwards.

To test his invention Blaise forced his brother-in-law to walk up a local mountain carrying the barometer. (The scientist's health wasn't up to making the climb himself, of course.) The climber found that the air pressure dropped as he went higher. The higher you go the less air there is pushing down on you. Today the brave brother-in-law is forgotten but pressure is measured in "Pascals." (1 Pascal = 1 Newton per square metre.)

Bet you never knew!
Imagine all those kilometres of air above you pressing down on your head. The air pressure on your body is an incredible 100,000 Pascals. That's the same weight as two elephants. Luckily, the air inside your body is under pressure too. It pushes outwards with the same force so you don't even notice it. Planes that fly at high altitudes have pressurized cabins in which the air is kept at the same pressure as ground level. If a pilot flew without this protection the lower air pressure would cause air bubbles in his or her body to get bigger. The guts and lungs would swell painfully and air bubbles trapped in fillings could make their teeth explode.

Dare you discover . . . how air pressure helps you drink?

You will need:

Yourself

A bottle of your favourite drink (it's all in the interests of science) – just so long as the bottle's got a narrow neck.

What you do:

1 Try drinking from the bottle. Sit upright and tip the bottle up so it's level with your mouth. You can easily suck the liquid up.

2 Now stick the mouth of the bottle in your mouth. Wrap your lips around the neck of the bottle. Now try to drink. What do you notice?

a) It's as easy as before.

b) You can't suck any more drink up.

c) You dribble uncontrollably into your drink.

Answer: b) Before you drink you breathe in. This lowers the air pressure in your mouth. The higher air pressure inside the bottle forces the drink into your mouth. By covering the mouth of the bottle you make the air pressure in the bottle the same as your mouth. The drink won't flow. Don't suck too hard or you might swallow the bottle instead. But it would have been far worse if there'd been a vacuum in the bottle. Here's why . . .

TERRIBLE TEACHER JOKE

WHY IS OUTER SPACE SO TIDY?

I'M ABOUT TO FIND OUT

BECAUSE IT GETS A 100 PER CENT VACUUM!

SHE'S GOT A VACUUM BETWEEN THE EARS

UNDER PRESSURE

1 The first man-made vacuum was made by Otto von Guericke (1602–1686) Mayor of Magdeburg, Germany. In his spare time Otto was keen on scientific experiments. In 1631 Magdeburg was destroyed in war and 70,000 people were killed, but Von Guericke got away and carried on researching.

2 In 1647 he tried pumping air from a beer cask. But more air got in and made a strange whistling noise.

3 So he put the beer cask in a barrel of water. Water was sucked into the cask with a strange squelching noise.

4 Next he made a hollow copper ball. But when he pumped the air out it was crushed by an unseen force.

5 In 1654 von Guericke made a hollow ball from two stronger copper cups and pumped out the air. He'd made a vacuum. The pressure of the air outside jammed the cups together. It was this pressure that had crushed the earlier ball.

6 Fifty men couldn't pull the cups apart.

7 Two teams of horses didn't stand a chance.

8 But when von Guericke pumped air into the hollow centre the cups fell apart.

SOME PRESSING FACTS

1 In the 1890s Aimée, a young circus performer, used the power of vacuums to walk upside down. Her shoes had suction caps attached to them and as she walked the air was pushed out of the caps. The pressure of the air outside the caps then glued her feet to a board hung from the ceiling. Very im-press-ive!

2 Champagne in a bottle is under pressure too. This is due to all the gas bubbles squeezed into the drink. When shaken and heated the cork fires at 12.3 metres a second – as fast as a rock blasted with dynamite. It definitely makes a party go off with a bang.

3 Pressurized liquid or gases are used in hydraulic machines, such as the powerful pistons that lift crane jibs. One early hydraulic machine was a nineteenth-century vacuum cleaner. Water was squirted one way and the falling pressure sucked in air and dirt behind it. But when water went the wrong way it flooded your home.

I THINK WE'LL STICK TO THE DUSTPAN AND BRUSH, POLLY

4 In 1868 American inventor George Westinghouse (1846–1914) made an air brake. It used the cushioning effect of air pressure to halt a train. Rail tycoon Cornelius Vanderbilt called it a "foolish notion." He didn't think air could stop a train. But nowadays air brakes are used on buses and trucks too.

Air pressure can do amazing things but can it also haul a train? It took a genius to see the possibilities in this "train of thought." A hard-driving, ruthless, workaholic genius in a black top hat.

Hall of fame: Isambard Kingdom Brunel
(1806–1859)
Nationality: British

Isambard Kingdom Brunel dedicated his life to engineering. He developed some spectacular engineering projects that used the forces of nature to help make people's lives easier.

He built railways, giant iron ships and tunnels on a grand scale. At times he was so wrapped up in his work that he showed little concern for others. He even sent his crippled son to a school where there were daily floggings. When the child complained, bossy Brunel snapped at him:

Issie loved to attempt the seemingly impossible. Sometimes he was successful but he also made many fatal mistakes. This story is about one of them . . . a railway powered by air pressure.

PIPE DREAMS
Devon, England 1848
Isambard Kingdom Brunel chewed on his giant-sized cigar as he strode angrily along the railway. As usual his mind was jumping with ideas. Fantastic ideas. Mighty plans. Pipe dreams. They had all seemed so easy. Once.

Four years ago Brunel and some other leading engineers visited Ireland to see the world's first "atmospheric railway." A railway where the carriages were pulled quickly and silently. Pulled along by the amazing power of air.

The idea was simple . . .

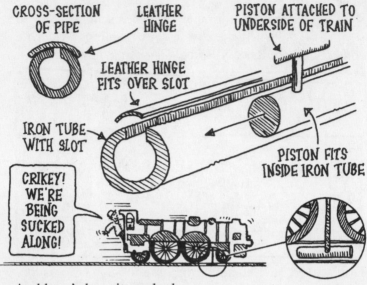

And here's how it worked.

1 Powerful steam engines pump the air from the pipe.
2 A piston travels along the pipe. It's pushed by air trying to rush back into the vacuum.
3 The piston is linked to passenger carriages and provides the moving power.

The other engineers laughed at the strangely silent railway. They thought it was impractical. But Isambard was quietly impressed. He suggested using atmospheric pressure for the South Devon Railway. But he forgot to mention to anyone that the Irish railway was always breaking down. Little old ladies rushed to sink their savings in a scheme backed by the world's greatest engineer. But the pipe dream soon turned into a pipe nightmare.

Now Brunel had come to see things for himself and young Tom the signalman's boy was showing him around.

"It's the leather hinges, Mr Brunel," said Tom slightly in awe of the great man. "They dry and crack in cold winter weather. And they rot in warm sunshine."

"So I see," said Brunel wrinkling his nose in distaste. "What's that appalling smell?"

"That'll be the fish oil. The railway pays people to walk along the line and paint the leather with soap and fish liver oil to keep it soft. Smells disgusting, it does."

They walked on until they reached one of the massive brick-built pumping sheds.

"Here's the other problem!" cried Tom. He nervously twisted his pale sweaty fingers. "It's the pipes . . ."

"What do you mean pipes?" bellowed Brunel above the noise of the engines. The huge steam engine snorted foul black smoke like an angry dragon. The gasping pumps sucked the air from the hollow iron pipes. And with the air came a stream of horrible things.

Oily water, rust and dead rats.

Rats. *Water.*

"How did they get there?" Brunel roared into the boy's ear. But he'd already guessed the terrible truth.

Hungry rats chewed the oily leather flaps until they were no longer air-tight. Water seeped in and rusted the pipes.

The famous engineer strode on furiously with the signalman's boy jogging to keep up. Suddenly Brunel bent down to touch the rat nibbled leather. Tom watched in fascinated horror. "No!" he shouted.

Brunel had his hand on the flap when Tom grabbed his arm.

"Stand aside boy!" ordered Brunel curtly.

"*Please* don't touch it," gasped Tom.

"Why NOT?"

Then Brunel saw the ghastly danger.

The vacuum inside the pipe wasn't 100 per cent. But it could still pluck his finger bones from their sockets. Scrunch, squelch, plop. No more fingers.

He backed off, muttering. There were some things even the great Brunel dared not do.

In February 1848 Brunel told the company the problems were almost solved. But seven months later he advised the directors to scrap the entire project. The little old ladies had lost their savings. And they were angry.

So how did Brunel make it up to them?

a) He offered to build a new railway for nothing.

b) He said he wouldn't send his bill for engineering advice.

c) He offered them a lifetime's supply of smelly fish oil.

FACTS ABOUT FRICTION

Newton said that a moving object would carry on moving forever if another force didn't slow it down. That force is called friction. People use the word friction to mean aggravation, anger or annoyance. Like a really bad day at school. And in the world of fatal forces friction can also often spoil your whole day.

Fatal forces fact file

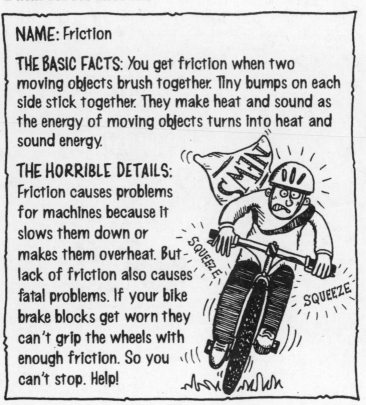

NAME: Friction

THE BASIC FACTS: You get friction when two moving objects brush together. Tiny bumps on each side stick together. They make heat and sound as the energy of moving objects turns into heat and sound energy.

THE HORRIBLE DETAILS: Friction causes problems for machines because it slows them down or makes them overheat. But lack of friction also causes fatal problems. If your bike brake blocks get worn they can't grip the wheels with enough friction. So you can't stop. Help!

SQUEEZE

SQUEEZE

Mind you, the man who discovered friction had an amazing life story. He could almost have been a character from friction – er, fiction.

Hall of fame: Benjamin Thompson (Count Rumford of Bavaria) (1753–1814)
Nationality: American

Ben Thompson was a teacher who escaped from school. He was born in the United States and besides being a teacher, he was a gymnast and a medical student. Until the war. The American colonists were fighting for their independence from Britain. But which side should Ben choose? The Americans or the British?

Rumour has it that he chose both. He spied for the British *and* the Americans. He was a sort of a double-agent. But the British never knew this and King George III gave Ben a knighthood when the war was over.

But Ben liked the excitement of being at war. He said he didn't want to "vegetate in England." So what did he do? Simple! He went to Bavaria as a special adviser on war to the government and became Minister of War in 1793.

As Minister of War, Ben devised a cunning plan. The streets were full of beggars and the army was short of uniforms. Ben's idea was to force the beggars to make uniforms. But how should he feed the beggars? After much research Ben found the cheapest food was watery vegetable soup. So he "vegetated" in Bavaria instead of in England – ha, ha. Ben was so keen on his idea he even published a book of recipes. Could this be a new line in school dinners? Then he had a second brainwave.

He put soldiers to work growing potatoes to make the soup to feed the beggars who made their uniforms. Ben's plan was a great success so at least it didn't land him in the soup! Brainy Ben made many other interesting discoveries. A new chimney for houses, a new stove and a coffee percolator to put on the stove.

And then he discovered friction.

One day Ben was watching a cannon being made. The barrel of the cannon was bored by a drill. Ben could feel the heat wafting off the cannon. In those days people thought heat was an invisible liquid. But Ben found you got extra heat if you used a blunt drill. So he figured the heat was produced by the drill. Dead right. The blunt drill had tiny bumps on its surface – and this caused extra friction. And more heat.

FACT OR FRICTION?

Often, just like Benjamin Thompson, physicists draw conclusions from things they noticed. Could you do this? Here are some everyday happenings. Which ones are caused by friction?

1 Friction helps you to build a house of cards.
2 Friction explains how you can whip a tablecloth off a fully laid table without breaking anything.

3 Friction makes electrical equipment heat up.
4 The patterns on tires causes friction with the road. This helps to control the vehicle.
5 People use friction to start fires.
6 Friction helps skiers to ski up hills.

7 Runners use friction to run without slipping.
8 Friction causes people to get burnt by snow.

Answers:

1 *Fact.* Tiny bumps on the surface of the cards help them to stick to the surface of the table. That's friction. It works if the cards are at a steep angle.

2 *Friction.* The inertia of the crockery and the force of gravity pins it to the table. If you pull the tablecloth fast enough there isn't enough friction to pull the crockery off the table. However, practising this trick at home may cause fatal friction with your family.

3 *Fact.* As the electrical current runs through the circuits it causes friction, which heats up the machine. That's why TVs can burst into flames if you cover their ventilation holes.

4 *Friction.* Smooth tires provide more friction in dry weather. The treads are better in wet weather. The wheel scoops the water out of the way so the tires can grip the road.

5 *Fact.* One of your ancestors hit on a hot method of lighting fires. Rub two sticks together. The heat of the friction can set fire to some dried fungus. Later on people found that partially burnt underwear caught fire again very easily. So it was ideal for getting a blaze going.

6 *Fact.* Traditional up-hill skis used sealskin for this purpose. Nowadays they have man-made bristles. It's kinder to seals.

7 *Fact.* Spiked shoes increase friction with the track.

8 *Fact.* Crazy skiers can suffer serious burns if they go too fast and then fall over. At high speeds, friction causes enough heat to burn the skin before the snow melts.

MESSED-UP MACHINES

Here's the bad news about friction. It slows machines down. Yes, it's a real spanner in the works for generations of freaky physicists who've tried to devise the ultimate machine. One that keeps on working without power. Perpetual motion.

Between 1617 and 1906 the British Patent Office received ideas for 600 perpetual motion machines. None worked.

Here are three more. Which one was successful?

1 A perpetual bicycle
The power for this bike comes from your bum bouncing on the saddle. This drives the rear wheel using a drive belt. So you could cycle forever, or until you get a sore bum.

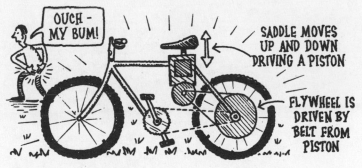

2 A self-powered pump

The water-lifting pump is powered by a waterwheel that is powered by water falling from buckets tied to the wheel as it runs around.

3 A perpetual wind machine

Dreamt up by an Italian doctor in 1500. Air from the fan is funnelled down a horn linked to a propeller which in turn powers the fan.

Answer: None of them! The fatal truth is that perpetual motion is as about as likely as a vegetarian vampire bat. And here's why . . .

A HOT HALT

Perpetual motion, unfortunately, breaks a law of physics. The Second Law of Thermodynamics to be exact. (Thermodynamics is the branch of physics to do with heat and energy. It's a subject you can really warm to.) The Second Law of Thermodynamics says that energy is lost from a machine in the form of noise, heat and, of course, friction.

So the machine stops because it runs out of energy. By the way, the First Law of Thermodynamics says you can turn energy from motion into heat. And it's true. Try rubbing your hands and friction turns the energy of your moving hands into a nice warm sensation.

A SLIPPERY SUBJECT

Sometimes we want friction. Brakes, tires, rubber-soled shoes, sandpaper and driving belts in machines would be useless without it.

THESE 'FRICTION' BOOTS ARE GREAT FOR WALKING UP STEEP HILLS!

But sometimes we don't want friction. We want things to go smoothly. That's why some slippery character invented lubrication. A lubricant, such as oil, fills out the little bumps that cause friction and allows the surfaces to slide past one another.

Most winter sports depend on lubrication. Sleds, skis and skates move easily because they melt a thin layer of ice beneath them. So they float along on this watery lubricant without too much friction. Until you slip over.

VERY LITTLE FRICTION

LOTS OF FRICTION

Lubrication also launches ships. That's why in the Middle Ages slipways were coated in revoltingly greasy animal fat. A slave got the risky job of knocking away the props under the ship. At the last minute the slave had to jump clear. If he slipped the ship would crush him – that's why they called it the slip-way. If the slave survived he was given his freedom.

But if lubrication is lethal, friction can be fatal. That was certainly the case in Rome four centuries ago.

FATAL FRICTION
Rome, 1586

It was an ancient obelisk. For 2,000 years it had lain forgotten in the dirt, west of St Peter's Cathedral. But times had changed. The Pope decided that the stone would look great in front of St Peter's. But how could it be raised? It was quite a problem. The obelisk weighed 327 tonnes.

"They say," murmured old Roberto, "that two engineers turned down the job. Reckoned it couldn't be done."

"I can see why," replied young Marco gazing in awe at the huge stone in its protective cage.

"Well – we'd better give it a try. Gotta earn our pay," grumbled Roberto with a wheezy cough. He and Marco were amongst hundreds of sailors hired to raise the obelisk. They took up their ropes.

The square was ringed by crowds. Thousands of people were cheering and waving handkerchiefs and waiting impatiently for the big event. A smartly dressed young man leapt onto a platform.

Roberto screwed up his creased old face in a scowl. "That's Fontana – he's the engineer who claims he can do it. What a big-head!"

"People of Rome!" proclaimed the young man. "Today we'll raise this great monument from the past. When the trumpet sounds you sailors must pull the ropes. Only stop when you hear the bell. It's vital that these signals are obeyed in silence. There must be no talking on pain of death!" The young man pointed sternly to the nearby gallows.

There was a shocked silence.

The older sailor made the sign of the cross. "That's a bit over the top," he whispered.

The sailors spat on their hands. The moist spit would help stop friction with the rope from burning the skin off their fingers.

The trumpet blared. The harsh note echoed around the square. Silently the men took the strain. The ropes creaked. Windlasses squealed. Capstans groaned around. Slowly, painfully the great stone began to lift.

Then the bell rang. Everyone rested for a few moments. The trumpet sounded again. Once again the sailors' muscles bunched and knotted until sweat trickled down their backs. Then disaster struck.

The ropes jammed – halted by friction between the ropes and windlasses. The sailors pulled the ropes until their faces screwed up in agony. Nothing moved. The taut ropes groaned and frayed. The stone tottered. Young Marco saw the danger. He shouted instantly: "Water, give water to the ropes!" Then he realized what he'd done. And knew he must die.

"Seize him!" screamed Fontana, his voice cracking with tension and disappointment. "Seize him for breaking the silence!"

Strong arms grabbed Marco. The guards dragged the young sailor towards the scaffold and the waiting executioner. The people gasped in horror but no one dared speak.

"I'm sorry," whispered Marco. But it was too late.

The executioner tightened the harsh hemp rope around Marco's bare throat.

A thin, old priest touched the sailor's arm.

"What's your last request?" the priest mumbled.

"Please, father," croaked Marco. His heart was racing and he couldn't speak clearly. His throat was dry and the rope didn't help. "Please, tell them to pour water on the ropes."

"I don't know if that's possible, my son."

"*Please* do it!"

The steel-helmeted guards beat their drums. It was the signal for the execution to begin.

The priest hurried over to Fontana. The young engineer nodded his head impatiently. A large water pitcher was found and its contents were poured over the straining ropes.

"Come on mate, let's get it over with," said the executioner cheerfully shoving Marco up the ladder of death.

Just then a trumpet blared and the ropes took the strain.

"Why are the people cheering?" thought Marco wildly. Were they pleased to see him die?

No. The ropes were moving easily. The stone was being lifted smoothly and quickly. At the foot of the ladder stood Domenico Fontana. Shamefaced.

"Release that man!" he shouted.

As a sailor Marco was used to hauling wet ropes at sea. He knew that there was less friction on wet ropes because the water acted as a lubricant. You'll be pleased to know that the brave sailor was pardoned and given his freedom. But what was his reward for saving the obelisk?

a) A golden pitcher of water.

b) Tea with the Pope.

c) His very own ship.

Answer: b) He met the Pope as a VIP guest. And the sailor's hometown of San Remo was given the honour of providing palms for the annual St Peter's Palm Sunday parade.

Well, hopefully you won't slip-up over this easy experiment.

Dare you discover . . . how to give things the slip?
You will need:

What you do:

1 Flick the bottle top along the first tray. Make sure the top stays on the tray and doesn't fly through the air.

2 Carefully pour a few drops of cooking oil on the first tray. Smear it over the surface with a paper towel until the surface is shiny and there is no extra oil on the tray.

3 Now flick the bottle top again as hard as before. Note what happens.

4 Mash up some of the banana and, using another paper towel, smear a little of it over the second tray. Make sure the surface is smooth and shiny and there are no lumps of banana left.

5 *(optional)* Mash the remaining banana with a little cream and sugar. Eat it. Tell your feeble-minded folks it's all part of the experiment. Who said science was tough?

6 Now flick the bottle top again as hard as before.

What did you notice?

a) Both the oil and the banana made good lubricants. They helped the top move faster.

b) The top stuck to the banana and skimmed along over the oil.

c) The top stuck in the oil but skimmed over the banana.

Answer: a) Lubricating oils are squeezed from peanuts, coconuts or bits of dead fish. In some countries bananas are used because they're slippery too. That's why you slip on a banana peel!

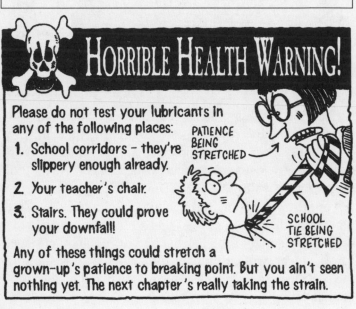

HORRIBLE HEALTH WARNING!

Please do not test your lubricants in any of the following places:

1. School corridors – they're slippery enough already.

2. Your teacher's chair.

3. Stairs. They could prove your downfall!

PATIENCE BEING STRETCHED

SCHOOL TIE BEING STRETCHED

Any of these things could stretch a grown-up's patience to breaking point. But you ain't seen nothing yet. The next chapter's really taking the strain.

STRETCHING AND STRAINING

Hold an elastic band between your fingers. Pull one end ever so carefully. The elastic band is storing the energy you put into pulling it. Let go – the released energy sends the elastic band flying. Oh dear – why does a teacher always get in the way? But just tell him that it's all part of a very technical scientific experiment – he'll understand! One of the first people to experiment with stretching was scientist Robert Hooke.

Hall of fame: Robert Hooke (1635–1703)
Nationality: British

After his bust-ups with Newton (see page 22), Robert must have known all about tension. But this talented scientist was interested in everything from telescopes to making flying machines that didn't fly. Incredibly, he also worked as an architect, an astronomer, a mechanic and a model maker. Yes. Hooke liked working at full-stretch.

According to one story Robert wrote a strange code in his will which deciphered into Latin reads "*ut tensio sic vis.*" Mean anything to you? Thought not. Further translated into English it means "as the extension so the force." And these weird words turned out to be Hooke's Law on stretching. Imagine hanging a weight on a spring – the spring stretches. Double the weight and the spring stretches twice as far. Simple, isn't it?

Dare you discover 1 . . . what happens when something stretches?

You will need:
Yourself
A 0.5-cm-thick elastic band

What you do:
Suddenly stretch the elastic band.
Put it against your face.
What happens and why?
a) The elastic band feels strangely cold because all the energy has been stretched out of it.
b) The elastic band feels warm. This is due to the energy that you have provided by stretching it.
c) The elastic band feels warm because stretching causes friction with your hot sweaty little fingers.

Answer: b) The band briefly stores energy from the force that stretches it. The energy tries to escape as heat and that's why the band feels warm.

Dare you discover 2 . . . the power of an elastic band?

Here's a machine that uses stored energy in an elastic band to get moving. Ask an adult to help with some of the cutting.

You will need:

SCISSORS
PARCEL TAPE
MATCHSTICK WITH HEAD CUT OFF
CANDLE
COTTON REEL
PENCIL
ELASTIC BAND

What you do:

1 Cut 2.5 cm off the bottom of the candle.

2 Remove the wick from the candle and make the middle hole large enough for the elastic band.

3 Pass the elastic band through the centres of the candle stump and cotton reel.

4 Pass the matchstick through the elastic band at its cotton reel end. Secure the matchstick with a strip of parcel tape.

5 Pass the pencil through the elastic band at its candle end.

6 Wind the elastic band by turning the pencil. Watch your vehicle creep along as the elastic band unwinds. Compare its performance on rough and smooth slopes.

What did you notice?
a) It climbed better on smooth slopes.
b) It climbed better on rough slopes.
c) It couldn't climb slopes.

Answer: b) The machine uses the force you put into turning the elastic band to move. The friction provided by rough slopes helps your machine grip the surface and climb better.

A STRETCHY SUBJECT

Here's some more elastic info to stretch your brain cells. A few hundred years ago in England, you could be sent to prison for a long stretch – stretched out on a timber frame with rollers at each end. This was the rack. The most anyone was ever stretched on a rack was 15 cm. After that their arm and leg joints popped out of their sockets. Rumours that racks were used in schools are just "tall stories." No – teachers just racked children's *brains*.

I ONLY PARKED MY HORSE ON A DOUBLE YELLOW LINE

In the 1700s rubber thread was used in clothes and underwear. Sadly, the rubber melted in hot weather and cracked in cold.

In 1839 scientists discovered a chemical treatment that stopped this from happening and rubber thread, known as elastic, was used in corsets and knickers from the 1930s. (Corsets are the tight-fitting garments some women wore to squeeze their bulging bodies into shape. Before elastic, corsets were reinforced with bits of whalebone.)

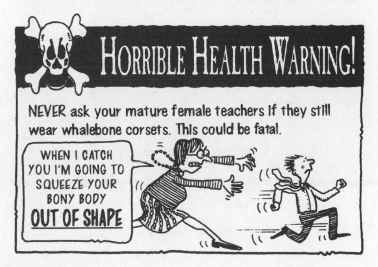

HORRIBLE HEALTH WARNING!

NEVER ask your mature female teachers if they still wear whalebone corsets. This could be fatal.

WHEN I CATCH YOU I'M GOING TO SQUEEZE YOUR BONY BODY **OUT OF SHAPE**

Nowadays man-made elastic is used for much more than just corsets – including the rope bungee jumpers use. Would you want to bungee jump?

If your answer to this question is "ARGGGGGH!" you wouldn't envy Gregory Riffi, who in 1992 jumped 249.9 metres from a helicopter over France. With his life hanging by a thread – all right – an elastic rope.

BY THE WAY CAPTAIN, I COULDN'T FIND ANY ELASTIC SO I USED ROPE INSTEAD – O K ?

By the way, bungee jumping isn't usually fatal if it's done by experts. But as the jumpers fall the blood rushes to their heads and this can make their eyeballs bleed a bit. Another sport that depends on stretching is archery.

BIG BAD BOWS

1 The bow was invented before 20,000 BC. The idea was that you could store energy by pulling back the string and transfer the force of the energy to fire the arrow.

2 Five seconds later the bow may have claimed its first victim. Ooops!

3 In the 900s the Turks hit upon a better bow. It was made from grisly bits of animal horn and tendons and strengthened with wood. The outward curve of the bow allowed it to be drawn with greater force.

4 Meanwhile the Europeans had invented the crossbow. This deadly weapon could fire a bolt 305 metres.

5 But the crossbow string had to be cranked back slowly. And during that time ordinary archers with ordinary bows were so skilled, they could turn a crossbow soldier into a pin-cushion in no time – unless he bolted first.

6 And then a Welsh person invented the long-bow. It could fire an arrow 320 metres. And straight through chain mail. At shorter ranges, the arrows could pierce armour too.

7 Modern bows are really high-tech.

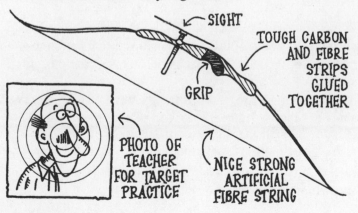

8 In free-style shooting the archers lie on their backs, strap the bows to their feet and draw the strings with both hands. Of course, it isn't only stretchy things that can store force. Springs can do this too when you push them down and then they pop up again. You'll be surprised to know that the earliest springs were used 600 years ago in mousetraps. And springs can spring real surprises on you. Here are seven more.

SEVEN SPRINGY SURPRISES

1 The first toasters, sold in 1919, had powerful springs that shot toast into the air. Bet that surprised a few people.

2 Springs sometimes break. Metal fatigue does in a cheap spring after about 100,000 extensions, but a better spring lasts over 10,000,000 extensions. A surprisingly long stretch.

3 Bed springs are a surprising shape. They're cone shaped – that's wider at their top than at their base. This makes them squeeze easily at first but the harder they're pressed the more difficult they are to squash. A bed that feels comfy and springy to you feels like a rock to a big, sprawling grown-up.

4 You know the circus act where a person is fired from a cannon? You may be surprised to discover that springs rather than explosions are used to provide the necessary force. The bang is a firework let off to make it look like the cannon had really fired.

5 And did you know we've got springs in our legs too? The ligaments that hold your joints together are a bit springy and your "S" shaped backbone jogs up and down as you walk. Together they'll put a spring in your step.

6 In the 1970s two American scientists trained a pair of kangaroos to hop on a treadmill. The scientists found that kangaroos jump using their springy tendons. It's a bit like jumping on a pogo stick.

7 Springy things are important for sports. Traditional tennis rackets were very expensive and strung with springy sheep's guts. Sounds like a bit of a racket. And talking about springy sports equipment, running shoes have to be springy too.

SUPER SPRINGY SHOES

HAS ANYONE SEEN MY RUNNERS?

SMELLY PONG

MIDSOLE ~ NICE SPRINGY BUBBLES

RUBBER LAYER – GOOD FOR PROVIDING FRICTION TO GRIP THE GROUND

Cut up your brother's runners like this and you'd better run for it before he takes a swing at you. Funnily enough the next chapter's about swinging and spinning too. Better stand clear.

GETTING IN A SPIN

Ever wondered why cars don't have square wheels? No? Me neither. Well – round wheels go around better (howls of amazement). Also the force on the outer parts of the wheel produces greater force at the axle. And this is ideal for wheel-based machines such as waterwheels and cars. And there's lots more wheel-life facts to go around (and pathetic jokes too) . . .

Fatal forces expressions

Who's to blame?

Answer: No one – his loonie is rolling away. He's describing how coins and any other spinning objects have a habit of turning until another force gets in the way. That's why wheels work so well. Best put your foot over the coin and pretend you haven't seen it.

And wheels **are** wonderful. They were invented by some bright spark who lived in the Middle East in about 3500 BC. When a wheel goes around, centripetal force tries to pull it towards its centre – remember that force from page 33? And now let's face a few more facts to get your head spinning . . . Oh go on – give it a whirl!

NAME: Centripetal force

THE BASIC FACTS:
Imagine whirling a
small ball round your
head on a bit of string.

1. Centripetal force tries
to move the ball towards the
centre of its spin.

2. When you let go, the ball's momentum sends it
flying off at an angle in a straight line.

O.K. – SO I NEED TO PRACTICE A BIT MORE...

THE HORRIBLE DETAILS: A bolas
uses centripetal force for catching
animals or people. It's two balls
on a rope. You whirl the bolas
above your head and let go. The
rope winds around your target's
legs. Here's how to make
your own.

HANG ON WHAT DID
YOU SAY ABOUT
CENTRIPETAL FORCE?

If centripetal force is making you dizzy, this rhyme might help you . . .

Centripetal's in a spin
All the time it's pulling in
Let go the string – it's worth a try
In a straight line it will fly

Dare you discover . . . how a bolas works?

You will need:
Two balls of Blu tack (adhesive putty) each 2.5 cm across
A piece of strong string or twine 52 cm long

What you do:
1 Wrap a ball of Blu tack around each end of the string.
2 Squeeze the Blu tack to make sure it is holding the string securely.
3 Now you can practise throwing it. Hold the string between your thumb and fingers, halfway between the two balls. Whirl the string around your head. Let go.

WHIZzzz

NOTE: READ HEALTH
WARNING FIRST ON PAGE 108

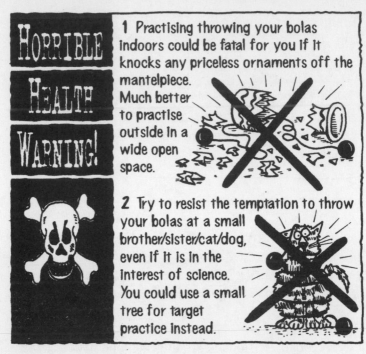

HORRIBLE HEALTH WARNING!

1 Practising throwing your bolas indoors could be fatal for you if it knocks any priceless ornaments off the mantelpiece. Much better to practise outside in a wide open space.

2 Try to resist the temptation to throw your bolas at a small brother/sister/cat/dog, even if it is in the interest of science. You could use a small tree for target practice instead.

From your observations how did the bolas work?

a) Centripetal force made the bolas fly straight. When the force stopped, it wrapped around the tree trunk.

b) The bolas flew straight until centripetal force did the wrapping.

c) Centripetal force made the bolas come back like a boomerang.

Answer: b) When you released the string, the momentum of the bolas made it fly off in a straight line in the direction it was heading when you let go. When it hit the tree, centripetal force on the string wraped the bolus around the trunk.

Going around in circles

Together centripetal force and momentum keep the show on the road and ensure that wheels are an all-around success story. They're useful for cars and trains, and buses and bikes, and tractors and windmills, and capstans that raise anchors. And thousands of other things too. Here are some amazing uses for wheels.

Weird wheels

1 The big Ferris wheels you see at fairs were first invented in Russia in the 1600s. They're said to be inspired by the custom of giving children rides in the wheels used to scoop water from rivers. If the wheels went around too, fast the children would be thrown into the river.

REVOLVING RUSSIANS

ARGHHHH!

RUSHING RUSSIAN RIVER

2 The name actually comes from American showman George Ferris who built a 75-metre wheel in 1893. Trouble is it took twenty minutes to go around once. Sounds as thrilling as watching porridge cool.

3 Wacky inventor Joseph Merlin gate-crashed a London party to show off the roller skates he'd just invented. The eighteenth-century scientist glided along playing his violin and feeling dead cool as he swished across the polished floor. Until he found he couldn't stop and crashed into a mirror. Merlin's problem was that his wheels spun easily on the smooth floor. And there wasn't much friction to slow them down. Bet he was really cut up about it.

PERHAPS ON REFLECTION, THEY'RE NOT SUCH A BRILLIANT INVENTION

4 By turning a wheel you can produce a force that can be used to power all kinds of machines. In the nineteenth century prisoners were put on the treadmill. They had to climb a revolting revolving wheel but they never reached the top because the wheel kept turning towards them. In the rotting prison ships the treadmills operated the pumps that stopped the ship sinking!

IT'S THE HAMSTER FOOD THAT REALLY GETS ME DOWN

Bet you never knew!

Remember the imaginary force from page 33? As the scientist cycled around the corner she felt as if a force was trying to throw her outwards. Some people wrongly think this is a real force called "centrifugal force." They imagine the force making a lasso fly thorough the air in a cowboy movie. Well, sorry folks – it doesn't really exist!

TEST YOUR TEACHER

This is such a simple test that even a teacher ought to get 50 per cent right – just by guessing – 'cos there are only two possible answers: **a)** centripetal force or **b)** the effect of momentum making something move in a straight line. Easy – isn't it?

1 It's used in labs to separate red blood cells from the rest of the blood.

2 The reason a pendulum swings more slowly in Central Africa than in Europe. (This is true.)

3 It helps your bike go around a corner.

4 The reason that you can whizz upside down on a roller coaster and not fall out even if you aren't strapped in.

5 The reason why a spacecraft doesn't fall to Earth.

6 You'll find this inside a rotor. That's the theme park ride that whirls you around as the floor drops away leaving you stuck to the wall.

TEACHER'S TEA-BREAK TEASER

If you are feeling madly brave, knock on the staffroom door. When it groans, creaks or scrapes open, smile sweetly at your teacher and say:

> EXCUSE ME, I WAS WONDERING WHY WHEN YOU STIR YOUR TEA, THE TEA LEAVES SETTLE AT THE CENTRE OF THE BOTTOM OF YOUR TEA CUP? SURELY THE TEA LEAVES SHOULD MOVE TOWARDS THE SIDES OF THE CUP?

Answer: Incredibly two of the world's greatest scientists puzzled over this for years. That's Nobel prize winners Albert Einstein (1879–1955) and Erwin Schrödinger (1887–1961). In 1926 Mrs S asked Erwin the question but he didn't know the answer. So she asked Einstein. After many calculations Einstein worked out the answer and even wrote an article about it in 1933.

According to Einstein, momentum does move the tea leaves towards the sides of the cup. But friction between the liquid and the sides slows down the tea leaves at the sides and base of the cup. As the liquid stops turning the leaves fall towards the centre of the cup. Wow! And you thought it was just a cup of tea! Here's another amazing story to keep things swinging.

114

GETTING IN THE SWING

It was 1586 and 17-year-old Galileo (yes, him again) was in Pisa Cathedral listening to a boring sermon. He noticed a chandelier swinging in the breeze. Sometimes it swung in a long arc and sometimes in a shorter swing. But each swing seemed to take the same time.

So Galileo timed the swings using his pulse. He was right. (Could you make a similar discovery during a boring science lesson?)

Galileo used this newly discovered fact to design a new kind of clock. The grandfather clock used a swinging pendulum to keep time. What a time-ly invention.

In 1650 two priests spent a whole day counting the swings of a pendulum in a bid to prove the pendulum really did keep time. It did and they counted 87,998 swings.

But one sickly scientist had even bigger pendulum plans.

Hall of fame: Jean Bernard Léon Foucault
(1819–1868) Nationality: French

Young Jean was a sickly child. And his parents reckoned school would finish him off, so they educated him at home. Why can't all parents be so considerate? Poor Jean was never any good at his lessons. For a time he went nowhere. His bid to become a surgeon failed after he ran away from an operation. One squirt of blood and a bit of suffering and wimpy Jean burst into tears.

But Jean loved writing. So he became a science journalist instead. Then he got interested in experiments. He measured the speed of light and tried to photograph the stars. He then became fascinated by the idea that you could use a pendulum to prove the Earth turned during the day. Although everyone knew this, no one had ever tried to prove it actually happened.

In 1851 Jean devised an amazing test. He hung a huge steel ball 60 cm in diameter and weighing 30.4 kg from the dome of the Pántheon in Paris, a large building where many famous people were buried.

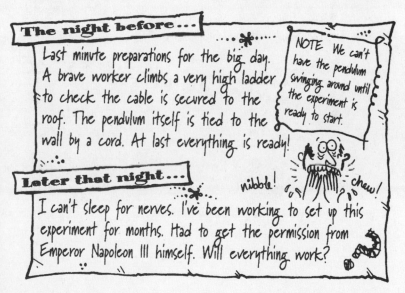

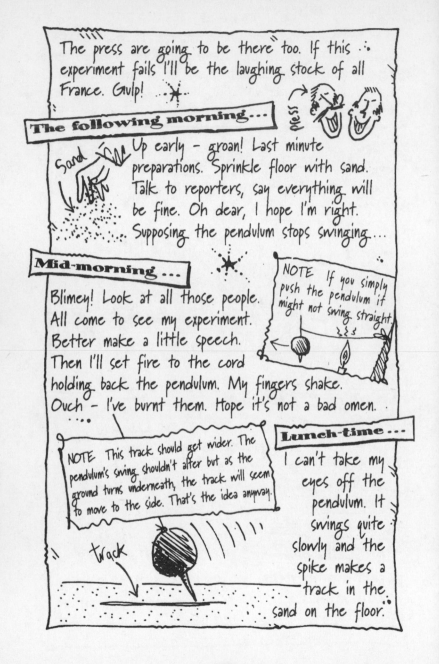

The press are going to be there too. If this experiment fails I'll be the laughing stock of all France. Gulp!

The following morning...

Sand

Up early – groan! Last minute preparations. Sprinkle floor with sand. Talk to reporters, say everything will be fine. Oh dear, I hope I'm right. Supposing the pendulum stops swinging...

Mid-morning...

NOTE If you simply push the pendulum it might not swing straight.

Blimey! Look at all those people. All come to see my experiment. Better make a little speech. Then I'll set fire to the cord holding back the pendulum. My fingers shake. Ouch – I've burnt them. Hope it's not a bad omen.

NOTE This track should get wider. The pendulum's swing shouldn't alter but as the ground turns underneath, the track will seem to move to the side. That's the idea anyway.

track

Lunch-time...

I can't take my eyes off the pendulum. It swings quite slowly and the spike makes a track in the sand on the floor.

118

Still swinging. Time seems to drag. I count the swings. It's like counting sheep.
I'm dozing off. Yawn – should have got more sleep last night. Zzzzzzzzzz zz

An hour later . . .

Still swinging. Nothing happening. I should have known this right from the start. Maybe I could push the pendulum to one side when no one's looking. Help! The Emperor's glaring at me and he's really cross. I'M FINISHED. PANIC STATIONS!!!!

Nap III glaring

← Still sleeping

Just then . . .
I open my eyes. Phew! It must have been a dream. Everyone's pointing to the sand and talking. THE TRACK HAS GOT WIDER. I'M SAVED!!!
The world really does go around. YIPPEEEEE! I feel like dancing about and kissing everyone.

119

Foucault found himself a hero. He was awarded the *Légion d'Honneur* medal. He went on to invent gyroscopes . . . which work on the same principle as the tops as you'll see in a moment. And tops are top toys for freaky physicists.

TOP TRICKS

Physicists like nothing better than playing with their favourite toys. Well, according to them they're investigating forces. Oh, yeah.

CAN I HAVE A GO NOW?

LOOK, LOOK, I'VE DONE A REALLY LONG ONE!

FIRST PERSON TO DROP IT IS OUT

There are loads of toys that use the forces of spinning. Toys like, yo-yos, hula-hoops, Frisbees. And tops. A top was a favourite toy of Nobel prize winner Wolfgang Pauli (1900–1958) who was trying to work out the physics of inertia. Here's some crucial info to make *you* "tops" of the class.

Tops balance because angular momentum keeps them going – remember the coin running away from the scientist? Tops keep turning in the same way despite the efforts of gravity to pull them down. Bigger tops need more effort to get going but spin for longer. Tops are popular with kids the world over. Here's a traditional Inuit game you might like to play when it gets really cold.

You will need:

IGLOO   SPINNING TOP

What you do:
Spin the top. Run around your igloo (or house). Try to get back inside before the top falls down. (This could be fatal if you don't dress warmly first.)

YOU ONLY HAVE TO GO ROUND ONCE!

In 1743 English inventor John Smeaton (1724–1794) invented a sort of top that would stay level even on a ship in a storm. This allowed mariners to check where the horizon should be. They could then work out the positions of the sun and stars to navigate by. But the new-fangled top didn't catch on because seafarers were useless at spinning it.

But Smeaton's brainwave was the ancestor of the gyroscopes found on most ships and planes today.

Foucault's invention – the gyroscope – works like a series of tops. They balance on one another and always stay upright. This is ideal if you want to steer a steady course. Amazingly, your bike wheels work in much the same way. When they spin around the bike is much less likely tip over than when it's stationary. Scientists call this "precession." Something to think about next time you go for a precession on your bike.

Bet you never knew!

The tighter your circle of spin, the faster you go. That's why ice-skaters pull in their arms to spin faster. It's the law of conservation of angular momentum again. Because the circle of spin is smaller they go round quicker. This fact also explains why water speeds up near the centre of a whirlpool. You can check this fact by watching the dregs of your washing-up gurgle down the plug hole. And if this isn't your idea of fun you'd better dive into the next chapter. You'll soon get your bounce back.

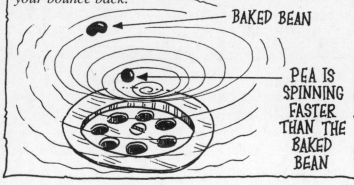

BAKED BEAN

PEA IS SPINNING FASTER THAN THE BAKED BEAN

BOUNCING BACK

What's always "around" for a game and doesn't mind a good kicking? No, not your sports teacher. It's a *ball*. And oddly enough balls do other forceful things. Like rolling and spinning and bouncing. Here are a few facts to bounce off your friends.

Fatal forces fact file

NAME: Bouncing

THE BASIC FACTS: When a rubber ball hits the floor the springy coiled rubber molecules that make up the ball are all squashed together. They soak up the energy of the impact and then bounce out again – making the ball bounce.

THE HORRIBLE DETAILS: The first chewing gum was made of chicle, a type of tree sap. American scientists tried to make the chicle into a type of rubber but it wasn't bouncy enough. So they just chewed the problem over, or rather chewed the chicle.

KEEP YOUR EYE ON THE BALL

When a ball flies through the air, strange things start to happen. Scientists have put loads of effort into working out what these mysterious effects are.

Fatal forces fact file

NAME: Flying balls

THE BASIC FACTS: When you throw or kick a ball friction with the air causes drag and this slows the ball. At the same time it's hit by turbulence. That's when spinning masses of air form around the ball and give it bumpy ride.

THE HORRIBLE DETAILS: A baseball can be pitched at 145km per hour (90 mph). That's fatally fast for anyone in the way without protective gear.

Any old scientist will tell you that ball games involve forces. So we invited a tame scientist along to show you how science can help you improve at sports such as tennis. According to the scientist you don't need to work up a sweat. All you need is a few brain cells and a small computer. *Oh, yeah?*

THE SCIENTIST'S GUIDE TO TENNIS

Tennis ball seams are the same on each side. This means equal amounts of air turbulence. So the ball flies straight. That's quite a velocity. Slice the racket downwards and you'll get back-spin. The ball tumbles backwards as it flies forwards. This drags air over it. As this air speeds up, the pressure above the ball drops and the greater air pressure under the ball raises it. We call this effect lift.

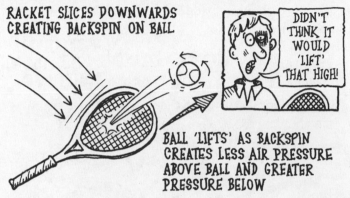

RACKET SLICES DOWNWARDS CREATING BACKSPIN ON BALL

DIDN'T THINK IT WOULD 'LIFT' THAT HIGH!

BALL 'LIFTS' AS BACKSPIN CREATES LESS AIR PRESSURE ABOVE BALL AND GREATER PRESSURE BELOW

Top spin is the opposite. Strike the ball upwards and the ball tumbles forwards as it flies forwards. This drags air under the ball. And as it speeds up the pressure drops and the ball is pushed lower and it bounces faster.

DIDN'T THINK IT WOULD BOUNCE THAT FAST!

RACKET MOVES UPWARDS CREATING TOP SPIN.

BALL BOUNCES FASTER AS TOPSPIN CREATES MORE AIR PRESSURE ABOVE THE BALL AND LESS BELOW

If you hit the ball a glancing blow it bounces extra slowly when it hits the ground. So it's even easier to whack.

PAINLESS PADDING
If you find games a pain in the sports bag maybe you need a bit more protection. Here are a few bits and pieces of equipment designed to help you play safe.

• Cushioned shoulder padding and shin pads as worn by football players.

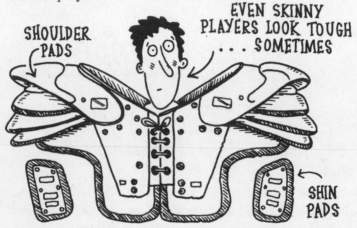

SHOULDER PADS

EVEN SKINNY PLAYERS LOOK TOUGH ... SOMETIMES

SHIN PADS

• Boxer's gum shield. Stops teeth from being knocked out of their sockets.

NO PROBLEM

• Football player's helmet. Cage to protect face.

CAGE TO PROTECT FACE

UNBREAKABLE PLASTIC

• Dome shape spreads force of blow over whole helmet. Stops head from getting squashed.
• Cricketer's box to protect the vulnerable bits. Very useful – cricket balls travel at 160 km per hour (100 mph).

HOWZAT!

PAINFUL!

WITH → BOX

WITHOUT → BOX

Here are a few more facts to prove that science really is a ball.

HAVING A BALL

1 The first balls were made by the Romans from bits of dead animal skin stitched together and filled with air.

Later on in the Middle Ages balls were made from pigs' bladders filled with air. Yuck – who had to blow them up?

IMPORTANT!
REMEMBER TO EMPTY THE BLADDER FIRST

2 The first golf balls were leather bags packed with boiled chicken's feathers. Bet that made the feathers fly. The balls flew very well until it rained when they soon got waterlogged and split. Covering the players in grotty old feathers.

3 In the 1850s someone had the idea of making golf balls out of rubbery tree sap. But they didn't fly as straight as the old balls until they became scratched and worn. Then they flew really well.

4 So what was going on? Turned out the rough surface of the golf ball trapped tiny pockets of air. The turbulent air flowed around the trapped air and this actually gave a smoother, quicker flight. And that's why modern golf balls have little dimples.

5 Cricket balls also do strange things as they fly through the air. Normally the ball just spins horizontally. But at speed, air turbulence makes the ball swerve if the edge of the ball's seam is smooth. That's why some cricketers polish the ball by rubbing it on their trousers.

6 At speeds of 100 km (62 mph) plus, the ball can swerve even more. Especially if the edge of the seam is rough. And that's why some cricketers rub dirt into the ball. But don't do this when you play – it's called cheating.

7 The ball used in rugby and football has pointed ends. If it's tumbling forward it can bounce oddly. Sometimes it bounces high, sometimes low.

8 This makes it tricky to pick up. And dangerous too unless you enjoy twenty giant people jumping on your head. The good news is that the ball is easier to throw. Pitch it with one end pointing forwards and it'll spin horizontally like an over-sized bullet. This means you can easily get rid of it before you get flattened. It's safer than just standing and juggling the ball . . .

Dare you discover . . . how to juggle?

Juggling is a great way to see how forces affect balls in the air. Tell your gullible folks you're doing your homework. Then you can have a bit of fun.

You will need:

Yourself

Something to juggle with. Three balls small enough to fit in your hands would be good. Or you could try rolled up socks

Plenty of space

A mirror

Safety note: When you are learning to juggle try to resist the urge to use your granny's priceless antiques, food (especially at meal-times), and living creatures such as hamsters, goldfish, small brothers and sisters, etc.

1 Stand in front of a mirror with your elbows tucked close to your body and your hands level with your waist. Place your legs apart with your knees slightly bent. Easy, isn't it? Are you ready?

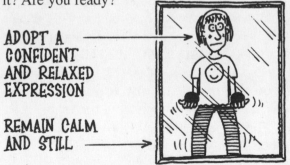

2 Take a deep breath and let it out slowly. That's right – relax. Now without looking at your hands . . . throw the ball gently up and over your head. Notice how it falls in an arc under the influence of gravity just like the cannonballs Galileo studied – remember? Catch the ball in the palm of your other hand. Keep your eyes in the top part of the ball's flight. OK – that's the easy bit.

3 Now it gets a bit harder. Juggling with two balls takes a bit of practice. Throw one ball up as before. When the ball is just about to drop, throw your second ball up from the other hand. Ideally the second ball should pass just under the first ball.

4 OK, this takes practice. Better practise now to get it right.

5 This is where it gets *really* hard. Three balls. Sure you want to try? OK. Hold two balls in one hand and one in the other. Repeat Step 3.

6 Now here's the clever bit. When ball 2 is just about to drop throw ball 3 up and try to get it to pass under ball 2.

Meanwhile catch ball 1 and throw it up just when ball 3 is about to drop. Easy!

7 Fantastic, keep going!

And while you're doing this, here are some interesting facts to juggle with.

1 The most balls anyone has ever managed to juggle was 10. This feat was achieved by several people, including American Bruce Sarafian in 1996.

2 Kara, a nineteenth-century German performer used to juggle with his hat, lighted cigar, gloves, newspaper, matches and a coffee cup. Don't try this at home . . . or at school.

3 It's also possible to juggle with your feet. This trick was pioneered by another American performer named Derious. As long as his back was supported, a performer could juggle quite weighty objects, even a small child.

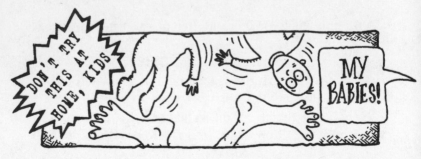

Sooner or later they'll invent a juggling machine. Then people could enjoy the fun of juggling without ever having to learn for themselves. That's typical of us humans. Always inventing machines to get out of hard work. There are loads more mighty machines that use forces to do work. Listen hard and you'll hear them grinding up their gears for the next chapter . . .

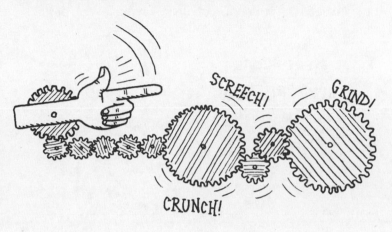

SCREECH!

GRIND!

CRUNCH!

MIGHTY MACHINES

A machine is a way of using a force in the right place to get a job done with less effort. Good idea. So why, after 10,000 years of science and invention is there no machine for doing homework? Anyway, to make a mighty machine all you need is a collection of effort-saving levers, pulleys and gears.

FATAL EXPRESSIONS

ARGH! ROTATIONAL INERTIA – I NEED MORE TORQUE!

Answer: No – she needs a mechanic. The scientist can't loosen a nut. Torque is the word scientists use to describe the turning force you produce using a spanner. Rotational inertia is the resistance of the nut to being turned. And spanners are good for doing this job because they work like levers, as you'll see.

LOVELY LEVERS

A lever is a pole that you use to lever something up or push or pull something around. Either way the lever rests on a point known as the fulcrum. Levers work because the most effective turning force is at right angles to the thing you want to move. So levers help you do more work for less effort. Lovely!

Dare you discover . . . how a lever works?

You will need:
Yourself
A door

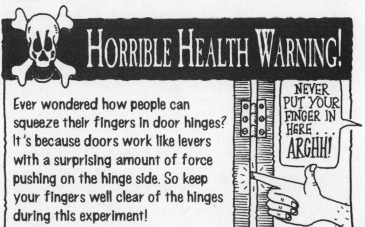

HORRIBLE HEALTH WARNING!

Ever wondered how people can squeeze their fingers in door hinges? It's because doors work like levers with a surprising amount of force pushing on the hinge side. So keep your fingers well clear of the hinges during this experiment!

NEVER PUT YOUR FINGER IN HERE . . . ARGHH!

What you do:

1 Open the door slightly. Make sure no one charges through the door.

2 Stand outside the door and try to push it by pressing with one finger 2 cm from the hinges.

3 Now press with the same finger 2 cm from the opposite side to the hinges.

NEAR THE HINGES

AWAY FROM THE HINGES

Which is easier?

a) They're both impossible and you got a sore finger.

b) It's easier to push the door near the hinges.

c) It's easier to push the door further away from the hinges.

Answer: c) The door works like a lever with the hinges as the fulcrum. You move the door further but at any moment you are using less force – so it feels easier. Nowadays you'll find levers everywhere – from typewriters to tin openers and from scissors to see-saws.

Bet you never knew!

You've got levers in your body. This interesting fact was discovered by the Italian artist and scientist Leonardo da Vinci (1452-1519).

Leonardo was cutting up human arms and legs in a bid to find how they worked. He discovered that muscles pulled the bones in much the same way as you pull a lever to move an object. He was so excited by this discovery that he even made a working model leg using copper wires and bits of real human bones. Then he could see it in action.

TEACHER'S TEASER

This playground puzzle spells break-time bafflement for your teacher. Two children are playing on a see-saw. If the little child jumps off she might get hurt. If the big child gets off he'll get a nasty injury as the see-saw swings up under the weight of the smaller child. What's to be done?

WHAT'S TO BE DONE?

FULCRUM

POWERFUL PULLEYS

Another method of lifting heavy weights off the ground – including large children – is the pulley. Basically it's a wheel hung off the ground with a rope passing over it. This re-directs force. So you can pull on the rope and lift something tied to the other end of the rope.

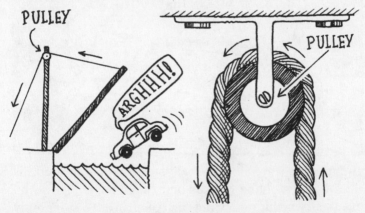

Add another wheel to the first one and it's even easier. By pulling the rope a longer distance you spread the effort so it seems easier to lift the load. Nowadays you'll find pulleys on cranes and lifts. So whom do we have to thank for this amazing invention? It was a Greek genius – Archimedes (287?–212 BC).

A LOVELY LITTLE MOVER

Archimedes had a little problem. His relative, Hieron, had asked him to pull a full-sized ship down a beach and out to sea – without help! Now most of us would tell the brother-in-law to jump in a vat of custard and go back to watching the telly. But Archimedes couldn't say that.

Unfortunately, Hieron was the local king – Hieron II of Syracuse to be exact. And you don't refuse royalty even if they are family. Besides, Archimedes was an all-round genius. He was supposed to know these things. He'd already worked out the math of levers and boasted that with a long enough lever he could lift the world. Hieron thought his brainy relative should be taught a lesson. So he deliberately set him an impossible task.

Archimedes scratched his balding head and chewed his lip. All that night he worked on mathematical plans. And eventually he hit on a solution. An answer so stunningly original, so forceful and amazing that no one had ever thought of it before. A new machine. Meanwhile, hundreds of grim-faced guards grunted and groaned as they hauled the ship up the beach. Hieron ordered them to load the ship with cargo and told some of them to wait on board.

Archimedes and a few assistants spent the next few hours setting up the machine. History doesn't record what it looked like. But it must have been a series of pulleys standing on wooden frames with the rope tied securely to the ship. When all was ready Archimedes gripped the free end of the rope. He looked rather thin and weedy. Hieron couldn't resist a quiet chuckle as Archimedes rolled up his sleeves and tugged on the rope.

But then the ship slid smoothly down the beach. It moved with eerie ease as if it was sailing on a calm sea. Archimedes' machine was a lovely little mover. The watching crowds gasped in disbelief. The people on the ship looked stunned and Hieron nearly had a heart attack. If he hadn't seen it with his own eyes the king would have accused his brainy relative of pulley-ing his leg.

GRINDING GEARS

No one knows who invented gears but the Romans certainly used them. They're interlocking toothed wheels that pass on force and they have odd sounding names that wouldn't be out of place in an ancient torture chamber. Names such as "bevels," "rack and pinion," "spurs" and "worms." They all work the same way. A smaller wheel that turns quickly and a larger wheel that turns more slowly.

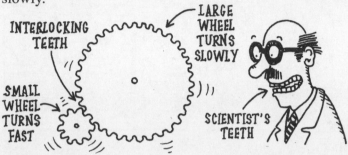

Gears increase the amount of work you get for the amount of force you put in. Take your bicycle gears, for example. The gear wheels on your bike have fewer teeth than the chain wheel. So the gear wheels turn faster and they make your rear bike wheel turn faster than you pedal. So it does you a really good turn.

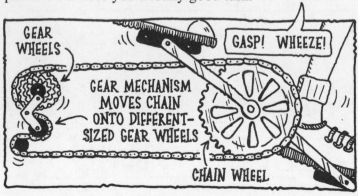

The bicycle was such a good idea that nineteenth-century inventors began to peddle their own pedal-powered machines. Which of these are too silly to be true?

NEW FROM *Real Victorian Value!*

PEDAL-POWERED PRODUCTS!

1. IDEAL FOR SHIPWRECKS

AMAZE YOUR FRIENDS AND ESCAPE THE SHARKS! THE PEDAL-POWERED LIFE PRESERVER.

COMFY AIR-FILLED RUBBER RING

PROPELLERS

SAIL - USEFUL IF YOU GET TIRED OF PEDALLING

LAMP FOR SOS SIGNALS

2. GET YOUR NAME IN PRINT!

WITH OUR TRICYCLE-POWERED PRINTING PRESS!

WE'LL CYCLE TO YOUR HOME AND WRITE YOUR MESSAGE ALL OVER YOUR FLOOR!

INK TANK

SOLID RUBBER LETTERS ON TIRES

3. DON'T MISS OUR BUS!

NO MORE SCHOOL BUS BREAKDOWNS. TRY THE NEW PEDAL-POWERED SCHOOL BUS. SPECIAL PEDALS UNDER THE SEATS LINKED TO A ROTATING CRANKSHAFT POWER THE BUS AT 35 KM PER HOUR (22 MPH).

"GETS THE KIDS TO SCHOOL ON TIME AND KEEPS THEM FIT."
I. FLOGGEM (HEADMASTER)

4. TIRED OUT?

RELAX UNDER OUR DELIGHTFUL PEDAL-POWERED COLD SHOWER!

ALL THE REFRESHING DELIGHTS OF GETTING CAUGHT IN THE RAIN WHILE ON YOUR BIKE!

A NEW AND EXCITING FORM OF EXERCISE THAT LEAVES YOU FEELING FRESH AND FIT.

PEDAL YOUR WAY TO A CLEAN BODY!

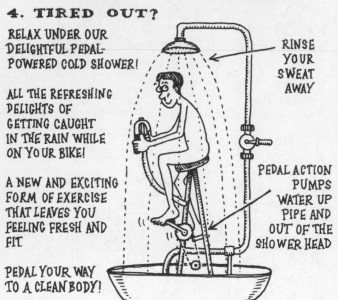

RINSE YOUR SWEAT AWAY

PEDAL ACTION PUMPS WATER UP PIPE AND OUT OF THE SHOWER HEAD

MARVELLOUS MIGHTY MACHINES

A complicated machine is simply lots of simple machines joined together. Easy. Just a load of old screws, pulleys, levers, gears, wheels, axles, chains, transmission shafts and springs that you just happen to find lying about in the garage. Throw them all together and everything should go like clockwork.

From bikes and gears it's a small step to steam engines, gas engines, trains, buses, cars and planes. Just think, if it wasn't for forces they wouldn't be able to force you to go to school. Terrible. Still, you can relax at home, can't you? No need to worry about forces is there? Safe as houses and all that . . . er – well, actually, forces *can* be fatal for buildings, too. The next chapter will really shake you up.

ACTUALLY, THE GARDEN COULD DO WITH A DROP OF RAIN

BUILD OR BUST

Fallen down under the influence of gravity, blown down, blown up or just shaken about. Yep. Forces are fatal for buildings, too.

BODGE-IT BUILDINGS

Some buildings stand for hundreds of years. Others stand for hundreds of days . . . or minutes.

Would you be interested in buying any of these structures?

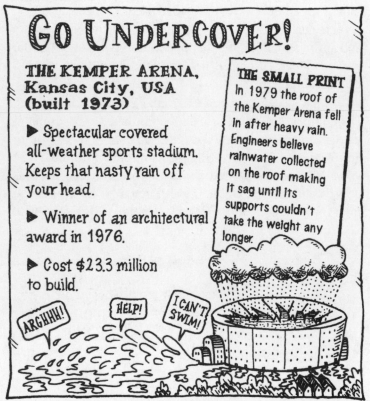

GO UNDERCOVER!

THE KEMPER ARENA, Kansas City, USA (built 1973)

▶ Spectacular covered all-weather sports stadium. Keeps that nasty rain off your head.

▶ Winner of an architectural award in 1976.

▶ Cost $23.3 million to build.

THE SMALL PRINT
In 1979 the roof of the Kemper Arena fell in after heavy rain. Engineers believe rainwater collected on the roof making it sag until its supports couldn't take the weight any longer.

ARGHHH!

HELP!

I CAN'T SWIM!

WAT-ER GREAT BRIDGE!

LONDON BRIDGE, Spanning the River Thames in London on 20 narrow arches. (built 1176 -1209)

DON'T DIG THE GRAVE THERE!

ARGHH!

▶ Waterwheels and shops.

▶ All this and the dead body of the architect, Peter Colechurch. He's buried in the chapel on the bridge.

▶ Sensational tidal surges through the narrow arches.

▶ Complete with drawbridge and spikes for traitors' rotting heads.

ROTTEN TRAITOR

THE SMALL PRINT

The arches were narrow and close together, and this forced the river to surge violently. This damaged the bridge and made life dangerous for boatmen. Up to fifty were killed each year trying to pass under the bridge. Part of the bridge fell down in 1281 and again in 1482. It was finally knocked down in 1832. Peter Colechurch should have designed his bridge with wider arches to allow the water to flow more easily. He should also have banned buildings on the bridge itself because their weight was too great for the bridge to bear.

Go With A Swing!

THE TACOMA NARROWS BRIDGE, Washington State, USA (built 1940)

▶ A graceful lightweight suspension bridge. (That's a bridge supported by cables hung from towers.)

▶ Amazing 853-metre span.

▶ Swings about in the wind for a really exciting crossing.

THE SMALL PRINT

The Tacoma Narrows Bridge swayed so violently in the wind that it earned the nickname "Galloping Gertie." People actually felt seasick crossing it. The bridge had to be reinforced to stop the swaying spreading to the towers that held up the cables. But four months later a strong wind twisted the roadway sideways until it collapsed.

BECOME AN ARCHITECT IN SIX EASY LESSONS
LESSON 1: UNDERSTAND THE EFFECT OF FORCES ON YOUR BUILDING

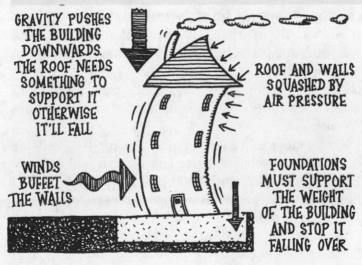

GRAVITY PUSHES THE BUILDING DOWNWARDS. THE ROOF NEEDS SOMETHING TO SUPPORT IT OTHERWISE IT'LL FALL

ROOF AND WALLS SQUASHED BY AIR PRESSURE

WINDS BUFFET THE WALLS

FOUNDATIONS MUST SUPPORT THE WEIGHT OF THE BUILDING AND STOP IT FALLING OVER

Nowadays architects make computer simulations and models of their buildings and even test the models in wind tunnels.

LESSON 2: DEVELOP AN EYE FOR FORCES

A good architect or engineer can look at a building and spot whether the building is well built enough to stand up to the forces on it. Marc Brunel (that's Isambard's dad) once looked at a bridge in Paris and said:

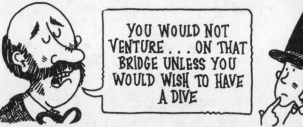

YOU WOULD NOT VENTURE . . . ON THAT BRIDGE UNLESS YOU WOULD WISH TO HAVE A DIVE

Three days later, the bridge collapsed. Yep, old Marc kept dry and he certainly had a dry sense of humour too.

LESSON 3: PUT IN PROPER FOUNDATIONS

If you've ever tried to carry some tall glasses on a tray one-handed like a waiter, you'll know how tricky it is to balance them. It would help if the glasses were partly buried in a really thick tray. That's how foundations work. The taller the building the deeper the foundations you need.

Foundations stop the wind from blowing your building over and they support the weight of your building too. Remember Galileo working at Pisa University? In 1173 Pisa's bell tower was built on soft ground with foundations that weren't broad enough to support its weight. Now Pisa University's famous for its learning and the tower's famous for its leaning.

LESSON 4: ALWAYS BUILD YOUR BUILDING THE RIGHT SHAPE

Triangles are a good strong shape. That's why the Egyptian pyramids have lasted 4,700 years. The Eiffel Tower was also made up of a series of triangles and many modern skyscrapers use triangles as the basis of their metal frames.

A column is a good strong shape and ideal for holding up heavy weights. Like the roof, for example. You can use arches to hold up part of the walls. Like columns, arches are great because the harder you push down on them the more they push back. Yes – it's Newton's Third Law again.

Dome shapes are also very strong. But you knew that from finding out about helmets in Chapter 9. An egg shape is also surprisingly strong and can take a weight of 22.7 kg. But don't try leaving an egg on your teacher's chair.

LESSON 5: MAKE SURE YOUR WALLS DON'T FALL DOWN

If you are designing a very tall stone building you may choose to make your walls very thick like an old cathedral or castle – the walls of the Tower of London are more than 4.6 metres thick. So you want to put in larger windows but you know they will weaken your walls? No problem. Try using buttresses to hold your walls up.

Mind you, disasters do happen. In 1989 the Civic Tower in Pavia, Italy (built 1060) fell with a crash. The cement holding the stones together had slowly crumbled away. Engineers reckoned that the shock waves from years of ringing the bells at the top had brought on the destruction. If this puts you off building in stone you could use a strong steel frame for your tall building and use lighter materials for your walls. This makes them stronger but the building might sway a bit in windy weather.

LESSON 6: GET YOUR ROOF THE RIGHT SHAPE

Roofs are usually sloping because the curved shape is more difficult to bend. You can prove this by holding a piece of paper in different ways.

HOLD IT LIKE THIS AND IT'S FLOPPY

BUT HOLD THE PAPER LIKE THIS AND ITS STRAIGHT.

VICIOUS VIBES

One thing that can be very destructive is vibration. Have you ever watched a washing machine shuddering and shaking as it washes and spins the clothes. Perhaps you've bravely laid a finger on the machine and felt the shaking passing up your arms. These are vibrations. And beware. They can be vicious.

TRAPPING YOUR TIE COULD PROVE FATAL...

Should you dial 911? No, her car's shuddering with vibrations. Probably because it's so run down. Oscillatory motion is in fact what vibrations are called. Oscillations are regularly repeated movements or shaking. The only way to stop them is to "damp them down." No, this doesn't mean chucking water over the car. Still confused? Well, it means using some soft substance to absorb the vibrations and stop the shuddering.

VICIOUS VIBRATION FACTS
Vibrations are particularly vicious in their effects on buildings and bridges. In 1850, 487 soldiers were marching across a suspension bridge in Algiers in Africa. Their heavy boots thudded on the roadway. And soon the whole bridge was shaking with the vibrations. It shook so much that bits fell off it and finally the entire bridge collapsed into the river. Tragically, 226 soldiers were killed.

Ever since, soldiers avoid marching in step when they cross a bridge in order not set off the deadly vibrations. That takes a bit of foresight but sometimes it pays to plan the crossing of your bridges before you come to them.

Mind you, the most vicious vibrations aren't caused by people – they're caused by the Earth itself.

Every year there are hundreds of earthquakes. Some of them are fatal for people. Movement of vast rocky areas deep under the ground trigger powerful vibrations in the form of shock waves that can destroy entire cities. The damage is done because shock waves make the walls vibrate so violently that the building falls down. Feeling a little shaky?

Dare you discover . . . how much your body vibrates?

You will need:

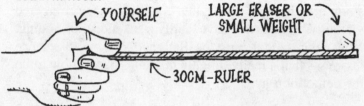

~YOURSELF LARGE ERASER OR SMALL WEIGHT ~30CM-RULER

What you do:
1 Place the eraser on the end of ruler.
2 Grip the opposite end of the ruler by your thumb and forefinger. Then hold the ruler as close to its end as you can.
3 Stretch out your hand balancing the eraser on the opposite end of the ruler.

What did you notice?
a) Nothing. I did the test for ten minutes and my hand was steady as a rock.
b) After a few seconds the end of the ruler began to dance around as my arm twitched.
c) I lost my balance and fell over.

A SMASHING FINALE

Now you've learnt about how forces affect buildings, let's practise using forces to knock one down. An old school will do. Imagine your school has been condemned as an unsafe building. Perhaps all those hundreds of feet stomping up and down the corridors have triggered vicious vibrations that have fatally weakened the building. Now your school must be flattened. No more science lessons – that's really tough. Oh well – here's how to do the demolition job . . .

1 Make sure that the school is empty of all pupils and there are no teachers lurking in the corners. You wouldn't want to knock the building down on top of them would you?

2 Start off by swinging a heavy steel ball against a wall of your school. The ball transfers its momentum to the

154

wall as it crashes into it. Cement is dislodged from the bricks and the wall falls down.

3 If you don't have a steel ball you'll have to smash the walls with a sledgehammer. This has the same effect but it's far slower and much harder work.

4 Some buildings have pre-stressed concrete beams. These are concrete beams with steel wires running through them. The wires are held tight by the weight of the building's upper floors. Be careful if your school has these beams. When you knock down the upper floors the wires in the lower floor's beams aren't held tight any more. So they go *ping* and the entire building crashes down around your ears.

Alternatively you could try one of these demolition methods.

Method 1.
Explosives

In a hurry? Want to knock your school down before science class on Monday? You could blow it up. Place explosive charges around the building and weaken the supporting beams so they collapse easily. Set off the explosives and wait for the dust to clear!

Method 2.
Hands

If you can't blow up your school, try using your bare hands instead. A karate blow is forceful enough to break bricks. In 1994 15 karate experts demolished a seven-room house in Saskatchewan, Canada using only their bare feet and hands.

MAY THE FORCES BE WITH YOU

Forces were around long before we got here. And although we try to use forces – in the end we can't control them. We can only forecast what forces might do to new buildings or cars. And although designers make fatal mistakes, these embarrassing slip-ups are thankfully rare.

Meanwhile, physicists are making more brain-boggling discoveries about forces. Before Galileo and Newton, no one knew how forces worked. Today we know more about them than ever. And because forces affect so much of our world, they pop up in every area of scientific knowledge.

Take atoms, for example. Scientists are probing how forces hold an atom together. (Atoms are the tiny bits of matter that make up everything in the universe.) The trick is to smash the atoms together in awesome machines called accelerators tens of kilometres long. Then you sift the debris for clues. If you're a scientist it sometimes pays to think small, ha, ha.

Forces also come into space travel. To plan a little trip around the solar system you need to know how a planet's gravity will pull your craft. And you need to be sure about what happens when you whiz around a planet and zoom off into the depths of space. So you'll be needing an advanced computer to cope with the necessary math.

Other physicists are looking into how gravity itself works. Are there really tiny things, even smaller than atoms, called gravitons that are somehow involved? And once scientists have found this out, could they perhaps defeat gravity and make planes that hover effortlessly in the air?

And even if we don't crack this one – there's always something new. Like a really wacky new sport. Take sky-surfing, for example. To do this you have to be seriously off your trolley. It involves jumping from an airplane strapped to a board. You enjoy some mid-air acrobatics before your parachute opens – assuming it does.

But one thing is certain – humans will go on pushing forces to their limits and scientists will go on studying how forces work. After all, there may be limits to our knowledge, but our curiosity knows no bounds. Yep. You're forced to admit it. Forces are horribly intriguing. Fatally fascinating. But that's Horrible Science for you!

FATAL FORCES

QUIZ

Now find out if you're a
Fatal Forces expert!

SCREECH!

GRIND!

CRUNCH!

To be a Horrible Scientist you need more than horrible habits. As every genuine genius knows you need brainpower too. The question is, having read this book have you got what it takes upstairs? (Don't decide until you've got to grips with this queasy quiz!)

Fun forces (these are the basic bits that even a teacher ought to know!)

Before we test your knowledge of fatal forces and see if you really can be a Horrible Scientist, let's see if you've understood the basics. Match the forces below with their mysterious meanings and effects.

1 Mass
2 Velocity
3 Acceleration
4 Friction
5 Energy
6 Momentum
7 Vibrations
8 Work
a) Changing speed or direction
b) The ability to do work
c) Keeps an object in motion
d) The amount of matter contained in an object
e) When a force causes an object to move a distance

ACTUALLY, THE GARDEN COULD DO WITH A DROP OF RAIN

f) Speed in a single direction
g) Carry force of impact away from an object
h) Slows moving objects

Answers:
1d; 2f; 3a; 4h; 5b; 6c; 7g; 8e

Fantastic forces quiz

So – reckon you've got the measure of forceful forces? Take this quick quiz and find out if you could truly be a freaky physicist . . .

1 Isaac Newton began investigating the force known as gravity when something fell out of a tree and hit him on the head. What was it?
a) An apple
b) A pear
c) A tomato

2 What would your terminal velocity be if you fell out of an airplane?
a) 9.8 metres a second
b) 50 metres a second
c) No one has been brave enough to try this experiment.

3 Why don't smooth golf balls fly as straight as pitted ones?

FASCINATING!

a) Smooth things naturally move in curves.
b) The pits create turbulence on the surface so the ball flies better.
c) The pits trap flies rather than allowing the flies to bump the ball off-course.

4 Why would a perpetual motion machine break the Second Law of Thermodynamics?
a) All machines lose energy in the form of sound, heat and friction. The machine would run out of energy.
b) Any machine that ran for ever would over-heat and melt.
c) A perpetual motion machine would be bound to run out of spare parts sooner or later.

5 Which of the following can be defined by gravity?
a) The force of attraction between two cars
b) The force of attraction between two tennis balls
c) The force of attraction between two people in love.

6 How heavy is the Moon (to the nearest few kilograms)?
a) 73,490,000,000,000,000 million kg
b) 1.5 kg
c) 597,420, 000,000,000,000,000 million kg

7 When an astronaut is out in space, what happens to his body size?
a) He grows several centimeters.
b) He shrinks a few centimeters.
c) He doubles in size.

8 What kind of apple did Isaac Newton get hit on the head with?
a) Flower of Kent
b) Allington Pippin
c) Golden Delicious

Answers:
1a; 2b; 3b; 4a; 5 – all of the above (every object with mass has a gravitational pull); **6a; 7a; 8a**

Force fact or fiction

There are still many misleading myths about fatal forces. Can you figure out which of these silly statements are totally true and which are forcefully false?

1 Archimedes managed to move an entire ship by himself using a pulley system.

2 The longbows used in medieval times were capable of firing an arrow further than a kilometre.

OH YES, VERY FUNNY

3 In 1996 Bryan Berg built a card tower 13.96 metres high.

4 The furthest a man has been fired out of a cannon using an explosive charge is 87.5 metres.

5 It is possible to create fire by rubbing two sticks together.

6 The gravitational pull at the Equator is stronger than it is at the North Pole.

7 The pressure you would feel at the deepest point of the ocean is equivalent to two men standing on your head.

8 Water can be made to boil at 40° Celsius.

Answers:
1 True.
2 False. The arrow could only travel 320 metres – but that was still far enough to injure an enemy before he got to you!
3 False. Bryan's card tower was only 7.86 metres high. Mind you, that's quite a height if you were on top of it.
4 False. To propel a human cannon ball they don't use explosives – they use a very strong spring!
5 True. The friction creates enough heat for it to start to smoke. And where there's smoke there's fire . . .
6 True. Because the Earth bulges out slightly at the Equator it is further from the centre and this makes the gravitational pull a bit weaker at the poles.
7 False. It's the equivalent of an average person balancing 48 jumbo jets on their head!

8 True. If the pressure is high enough, the water will boil.

Speed, pressure and temperature

You can't escape forces on Earth – or even in space! Speed, pressure and temperature and three of the effects of forceful forces that physicists find fearfully fascinating. But how much do you know about them?

1 How much gravity is there at the centre of the Earth? (Clue: It's nothing to worry about.)

2 Why do super-speedy cyclists wear funny-shaped helmets? (Clue: Oh, what's the point?!)

3 What happens to your lungs as you dive deep under water (Clue: Take a deep breath now)

4 What would happen if you accelerated at a force of 9 g? (Clue: This one's dead easy)

5 Why did trains have cow catchers? (Clue: think of a flying cow)

6 Where was the lowest temperature recorded on Earth? (Clue: Don't go "Russian" into this answer)

7 Is the acceleration due to gravity on the Moon more or less powerful than it is on Earth? (Clue: Floating free)

8 A person standing in high heels on a floor exerts a massive pressure on a small point. How many elephants would that pressure be equivalent to? (Clue: It'd be standing on tiptoe . . .)

Answers:

1 None. The force of gravity doesn't exist at the Earth's core – but you don't really want to go there to see if I'm right!

2 The pointed front on the helmet makes the air move around them rather than bumping into them and slowing them down.

3 They get squashed – more and more so as the pressure increases the deeper you go.

4 A force of 4 to 6 g managed for only a few seconds before you'd pass out (or your eyes would start to bleed). At 9 g you'd be dead!

5 They scooped buffalo out of the way of the train.

6 It was recorded in Russia – a bone-chilling -89.4°C.

7 Less. The gravitational pull on the surface of the Moon is 1.62 metres per second squared. This is only about one-sixth of that on Earth.

8 Just one – but it would be standing on one foot!

Freaky physicists

Over the years, strange scientists have conducted many evil experiments and come up with hundreds of ingenious inventions to learn about fatal forces. Can you identify the freaky physicist by what they might have said?

1 "Ow! That will leave a bump!"
2 "Can I have my balls back please?"
3 "Everyone thinks I'm full of hot air!"
4 "I've been under a lot of pressure recently."
5 "I'm in the swing of it"
6 "This invention really sucks!"
7 "Pass me that screw, will you?"
8 "You spin me right round . . . la la la."

a) Blaise Pascal
b) Otto von Guericke
c) Isaac Newton
d) George Ferris
e) Archimedes
f) Galileo Galilei
g) Jean Foucault
h) Isambard Kingdom Brunel

I'VE BEEN UNDER A LOT OF PRESSURE RECENTLY

Answers:

1 c) Isaac Newton discovered gravity when an apple fell on his head.

2 f) Galileo used balls to experiment with gravity.

3 a) Pascal invented the barometer – a device to measure air pressure.

4 h) Among other things, Brunel invented a train that was powered by atmospheric pressure.

5 g) Foucault did some amazing experiments with his pendulum.

6 b) Von Guericke invented the vacuum pump.

7 e) Ancient Archimedes invented the machine known as the screw or screwpump.

8 d) Ferris invented the Ferris wheel – well, what did you think he invented the mini-roundabout?

HORRIBLE INDEX

acceleration (changing speed/direction) 32, 61

aerodynamic shapes 38

air pressure 69–79, 125, 147

airbags 45

aircraft 46–51

Alexander the Great (king of Macedonia) 27

apple core, most famous 15

archery 100–2

arches
in dams 147
killing boatmen 145
pushing back 149

Archimedes (Greek inventor) 137–9

architects (building designers) 145, 147–8

Aristotle (Greek philosopher) 26–8

atoms, smashing 157–8

back-spin 125

balance 54, 68, 122, 148
counter 33
losing 31
wobbly 29, 65–8

balls 123–33, 154–5

barometers, invented 70

barriers, breaking 46, 48

bicycles (bikes) 28–34, 85, 109, 111, 122, 140–3

Blondin, Jean (French tightrope walker) 66–7

bolas (two balls on a rope) 106–8

bouncing 123–33

bows, big bad 100–2

bridges, building 145–6, 148, 152

Brunel, Isambard Kingdom (English engineer) 74–9, 148

Brunel, Marc (Isambard's dad) 148

bucket game 15

buildings
bodge-it 144–52
shaking 143, 152–7

bullies, dealing with 22, 31

bungee jumpers 100

buttresses, holding up walls 150

calculus, inventing 13, 23

canals, semi-circular 29

cards, house of 67, 83–4

cars 42–5, 105, 109, 143, 157

cats, sky-diving 55

centrifugal force, unreal 109, 111

centrifuges, real 113

centripetal force 10, 33, 105–9, 113

chemistry 23

chicle (tree sap) 123

coins
pyramids of 67
running away 105, 120

Colechurch, Peter (British architect) 145

columns, strength of 149

cornering 33

corsets, squeezing into 99–100
cow catchers 40
crumple zones 45

Da Vinci, Leonardo (Italian artist/
scientist) 136
dams, building 147
demolition jobs 154–6
Derious (American foot juggler) 132
domes, strength of 149
door hinges, fingers in 135–6
drag, such a 32, 38, 54–5, 124–5
drink, how to 71–2

earthquakes 153
Einstein, Albert (German-born
physicist) 114
elastic bands, power of 95, 97–8
electrical equipment 83–4
energy (ability to do work) 35, 86–7,
96, 100, 102, 123
engineers, energetic 42–5, 74–9,
89–92, 144, 148, 150
equator, bulging 113
executions, horrible 52, 56–7
experiments 12, 72, 116–17
    amazing 60–1
    easy 93–4
    poisoned by 23
explosions, dust from 156
eyeballs, plopping 72

Ferris, George (American showman)
109
fires, lighting 83–4
First Law of Thermodynamics 87
Foucault, Jean Bernard Léon
(French physicist) 116–22
foundations, strong 147–8
freefall parachuting 53–5
friction, furious 33–4, 79–94, 96, 98,
113–14, 124
frisbees 120
fulcrum (turning point) 134, 136–7

Galileo Galilei (Italian scientist)
59–65, 115, 130, 148, 157
gears, grinding 33, 140–3
George III (British king) 81
grasshoppers 27
gravitons, existence of 52, 158
gravity 5–7, 10, 16, 18–19
    centre of 65–6
    falling foul of 22, 29,
31–2, 49–50, 158
    gruesome 52–68, 112–13,
120, 130, 147
Guericke, Otto von (German
scientist) 72–3
guillotines, as toys 57
gyroscopes, invented 120, 122

hands
    demolishing buildings 156
    spitting on 90
hanging 56
heat 86–7, 96
heresy, heinous 63
Hieron II (king of Syracuse) 138–9
homework
    energy to do 35
    extra 13
    fun with 129
    machine for 134
Hooke, Robert (English scientist) 22,
95–6
horizon, where to find it 121
hula-hoops 120
hydraulics, pressured 74

indigestion
    dying of 27
    violent 70
inertia
    effortless 29–30, 120
    idle 40–1, 44
    rotational 134
Inquisition, dreaded 64–5

juggling 129–33

172

kinetic energy (used when moving) 31–2
knicker elastic 99

labs, untidy 34
laws 6–7, 18–21, 33, 39–40
    lousy 44, 86–7, 96, 122, 149
legs
    model 136
    springs in 103
    winding round 106
Leibniz, Gottfried (German philosopher) 23
levers, lovely 134–8, 143
lift, going up 125
light, containing colours 13
Locke, John (English philosopher) 22
lubrication, slippery 87–8, 92, 94

Mach, Ernst (Austrian physicists) 46
machines, mighty 134–43
mass 5, 30, 58–9
mathematics 5, 12–13, 16–17, 28, 35, 60, 138, 158
mechanics, amazing 134
molecules 69, 123
momentum 20, 30–1, 33, 38–40
    angular 105, 120, 122
    conservation of angular 105, 122
    momentous 106, 108, 111, 113–14
moon 13–16, 59
moose, loose 40
motion 80, 111, 113
    laws of 19–21, 39–40
    oscillatory 152
    perpetual 85–7
    theories of 26–35
mousetraps 102
moving *see* motion

nails, bed of 58
Napoleon III 117, 119

navigation (finding yourself) 121
Newton, Isaac (English scientist) 9, 11–26, 28, 33, 39–40, 44, 62, 65, 80, 95, 113, 149, 157
Newton's First Law 19, 33, 39–40, 44
Newton's Second Law 20
Newton's Third Law 20–1, 149
Newtons (units of force) 21, 70

obelisks, raising 88–92

padding, painless 126–7
parachutes 49, 51, 53–6, 158
Pascal, Blaise (French physicist) 69–70
Pascals (units of pressure) 70
Pauli, Wolfgang (Austrian-born physicist) 120
pedals 141–2
pendulums 10, 62, 111, 113, 115–20
Philip (king of Macedonia) 27
The Philosophiae Naturalis Principia Mathematica (Newton's book) 18, 23
physicists, freaky 34, 40, 46, 69, 83, 85, 120, 157–8
physics, laws of 6, 13, 34, 86, 120
pistons, powerful 74, 76
plague, deadly 13
planes 46–51, 70, 122, 143, 158
planets, moving 62, 65, 158
Plato (Greek philosopher) 26
Poe, Edgar Alan (American author) 10
potential energy 35
precession, while spinning 122
pressure, under 68–79, 125, 147
pulleys, powerful 137, 143
pyramids
    of coins 67
    strength of 148

racks, stretching on 98
railways, building 74–9
relaxing

173

at home 143
how to do it 130–1
resistance 134
rotors, whirling 113

safety belts, forgetting 42–4
Sarafian, Bruce (American juggler) 132
savings, losing 76, 78
Schrödinger, Erwin (Austrian physicist) 114
scientists 6, 65, 157, 159
driving cars 45
health of 70
not using slugs 59
riding bicycles 28–34, 111
running away from 120
smarty-pants 62
tennis guide 124–6
training kangaroos 103
seat belts, using 45
Second Law of Thermodynamics 86
see-saws 136–7
shape, importance of 149, 151
ships 88, 121–2, 138–9
shock waves 152–3
skin, burning 90
skyscrapers, building 149
slugs (American units of mass) 58–9
Smeaton, John (English inventor) 121–2
snow, burnt by 84
sound 46, 86
space, final frontier 37–8, 62, 72, 112–13, 158
spanners 134
speed 6, 19–20, 28–32, 35–51
smashing 60–2, 122, 128–9
of sound 46, 48
spinning 41, 105–23, 125, 128–9
sports, popular 53–5, 103, 126–9, 158
springs, surprising 96, 102–3, 143
squirrels, flying 55
steam engines 76–7, 143

strain, taking the 95–104
stretching 95–104

teachers 29, 72
teasing 114, 136–7
testing 16–17, 36, 59, 111
teeth
exploding 70
interlocking 140
knocked out 126
telescopes 62–3, 65, 95
tennis 125–6
tension 95–104
test dummies 42–4
thermodynamics (heat/energy science) 86–7
thermometers, inventing 62
Thompson, Benjamin (American scientist/spy) 81–3
top spin 125
torque (turning force) 134
towers, leaning 148
toys
guillotines as 57
top 120–2
trainers, springy 103–4
trains 74, 76, 143
treadmills, running on 110
tree sap
chewing 123
flying 128
triangles, strength of 149
tricks, top 120–2
turbulence, terrible 124–5, 128

vacuums, making 71–4, 78
Vanderbilt, Cornelius (American tycoon) 74
velocity, terminal 31, 53, 125
vibrations, vicious 34, 151–4

water pressure 69, 72, 145, 147
weight 50–1, 70, 96, 149
of buildings 147–8
crushed by 57

    evenly balanced 66
    lifting 137
    problems 59
    of rain 144
Westinghouse, George (American
inventor) 74
wheels 105, 109–10, 113, 137, 140
whirlpools 122
wind 146–8, 150
work (force making objects move)
35, 134, 140

Yeager, Charles (American pilot) 46
yo-yos 120